PENGUIN (🐧) CLASSICS

THE BERNARD SHAW LIBRARY

ARMS AND THE MAN

GEORGE BERNARD SHAW was born in Dublin in 1856. Although essentially shy, he created in his journalism the persona of G.B.S., the showman, satirist, controversialist, critic, pundit, wit, intellectual buffoon, and dramatist. Commentators brought a new adjective into English: *Shavian*, a term used to embody all his brilliant qualities.

After his arrival in London in 1876, he became an active Socialist and a brilliant platform speaker. He wrote on many social and political aspects of the day, from war to the "Irish question" to Socialism. When he undertook his own education at the British Museum Reading Room, he developed a keen interest in cultural subjects, leading to a prolific output of music, art, and theater reviews, as well as five novels and some short fiction.

Shaw remains best known as a dramatist and was closely associated with the intellectual revival of British theater in the late nineteenth and early twentieth centuries. His many plays (the full canon runs to fifty-two) include *Widowers' Houses*, *The Philanderer*, *Mrs. Warren's Profession*, *Arms and the Man*, *Candida*, *The Man of Destiny*, *You Never Can Tell*, *The Devil's Disciple*, *Caesar and Cleopatra*, *Captain Brassbound's Conversion*, *Man and Superman*, *John Bull's Other Island*, *Major Barbara*, *The Doctor's Dilemma*, *Misalliance*, *Androcles and the Lion*, *Pygmalion*, *Heartbreak House*, *Back to Methuselah*, *Saint Joan*, *The Apple Cart*, *Too True to Be Good*, and *The Millionairess*.

In 1925, Shaw was awarded the Nobel Prize in Literature. In 1939, he won an Academy Award for the screenplay for the 1938 film *Pygmalion*, and he is still the only Nobel laureate to win the Oscar. He died in 1950.

RODELLE WEINTRAUB, former assistant editor of Shaw, has edited *Fabian Feminist: Bernard Shaw and Woman*, *Shaw 5: Shaw Abroad*, and the Garland *Captain Brassbound's Conversion*. She has also coedited, with Stanley Weintraub, two dual volumes of

Shaw's plays: *Arms and the Man & John Bull's Other Island* and *Heartbreak House & Misalliance*.

DAN H. LAURENCE, series editor for the works of Shaw in Penguin, was literary adviser to the Shaw Estate until his retirement in 1990. He edited Shaw's *Collected Letters*, his *Collected Plays with Their Prefaces*, *Shaw's Music*, and (with Daniel Leary) *The Complete Prefaces*.

BERNARD SHAW

Arms and the Man

A PLEASANT PLAY

Introduction by
RODELLE WEINTRAUB

Definitive text under the editorial supervision of
DAN H. LAURENCE

PENGUIN BOOKS

PENGUIN BOOKS

Published by Penguin Group

Penguin Group (USA) Inc., 375 Hudson Street, New York, New York 10014, U.S.A.
Penguin Group (Canada), 90 Eglinton Avenue East, Suite 700, Toronto, Ontario, Canada M4P 2Y3
(a division of Pearson Penguin Canada Inc.)
Penguin Books Ltd, 80 Strand, London WC2R 0RL, England
Penguin Ireland, 25 St Stephen's Green, Dublin 2, Ireland (a division of Penguin Books Ltd)
Penguin Group (Australia), 250 Camberwell Road, Camberwell, Victoria 3124, Australia
(a division of Pearson Australia Group Pty Ltd)
Penguin Books India Pvt Ltd, 11 Community Centre, Panchsheel Park, New Delhi – 110 017, India
Penguin Group (NZ), cnr Airborne and Rosedale Roads, Albany, Auckland 1310, New Zealand
(a division of Pearson New Zealand Ltd)
Penguin Books (South Africa) (Pty) Ltd, 24 Sturdee Avenue, Rosebank, Johannesburg 2196, South Africa

Penguin Books Ltd, Registered Offices:
80 Strand, London WC2R 0RL, England

This edition with an introduction by Rodelle Weintraub first published in Penguin Books 2006

3 5 7 9 10 8 6 4

Applications for permission to give stock and amateur performances of Bernard Shaw's plays in the United
States of America and Canada should be made to Samuel French, Inc., 45 West 25th Street, New York,
New York 10010. In all other cases, whether for stage, radio, or television, applications should be made
to The Society of Authors, 84 Drayton Gardens, London SW10 9SD, England.

LIBRARY OF CONGRESS CATALOGING IN PUBLICATION DATA
Shaw, Bernard, 1856–1950.
Arms and the man : a pleasant play / Bernard Shaw ; definitive text under the editorial supervision
of Dan H. Laurence ; introduction by Rodelle Weintraub.
p.   cm.—(Penguin classics) (The Bernard Shaw library)
Includes bibliographical references (p.   ).
ISBN 0 14 30.3976 8
1. Laurence, Dan H.   II. Title.   III. Series.
PR5363.A88 2006
822'.912—dc22   2005056724

Printed in the United States of America
Set in Sabon

Contents

Introduction

Arms and the Man (1894) and *John Bull's Other Island* (1904) are the only Bernard Shaw plays that King Edward VII saw. He hated the first, loved the second, and misunderstood both. In 1894, at a performance at the Avenue Theatre in London, suspecting that *Arms and the Man* was mocking the incompetence of the British military, both Edward, then still the Prince of Wales, and his brother Alfred, Duke of Saxe-Coburg and Gotha, looked increasingly unhappy. The worried theater manager, Charles Helmsley, went to the royal box. "The man is mad! The man is mad!" the prince exclaimed. Afterward, from Buckingham Palace came a more moderate statement. "His Royal Highness regretted that the play should have shown so disrespectful an attitude toward the Army as was betrayed by the character of the chocolate-cream soldier."

No aberration, Shaw's chocolate-cream soldier, rather than being disrespectful, anticipated actual events. In 1899, during the Boer War, Queen Victoria sent Christmas boxes containing chocolate to her troops in South Africa. In the first year of World War I (the Great War), King George emulated Victoria, sending "Princess Mary" boxes containing chocolate (or tobacco) to the troops on the western front. American Army "Armour" rations in 1922 contained three four-ounce blocks of chocolate, and World War II emergency K rations contained three packets for chocolate drink and a chocolate bar. A half century after Queen Victoria sent chocolates as presents to her troops, Nazi Germany's Youth Corps trainees were given chocolates as provisions when sent out on ski practice. After the surrender to Japanese troops in 1942, the British, Australian, and Indian troops who were in Singapore were imprisoned in Changi Prison on the eastern part of the island. British prisoners of war, officers, and enlisted men of the Malaya Command headquarters organized a theatrical group that performed, among other plays, *Arms and the Man*. Many of the men strongly identified with the Swiss soldier, who says that no man can stand three days without sleep. It was something that many of the prisoners had experienced themselves.

The scene early in the play in which a young woman is surprised by a soldier entering her bedroom through a window awakened no delicious recollections for the prince. Thirty-three years earlier, when he was an incompetent cadet at Curragh, near Dublin, his helpful comrades had introduced a willing young woman to his bed. Now a field marshal, courtesy of his mother, Queen Victoria, and with a plethora of lovely ladies eager to share his royal bed, he could not imagine a soldier who preferred chocolates to cartridges and a bed for sleeping rather than for dalliance.

Nor did it occur to the future king that the play was as much about pathetically underdeveloped countries like Ireland as it was about a recent, if obscure, Balkan war. However much the play satirized impossibly romantic views of war and love, it was also about what Shaw called the predicament of people (in the play, the Bulgarians) "redeemed from centuries of miserable bondage . . . beginning to work out their own redemption from barbarism—or, if you prefer it, beginning to contract the disease of civilisation. . . . And their attempts at Western civilisation were much the same as their attempts at war— instructive, romantic, ignorant. They were a nation of plucky beginners in every department."

The notebook containing Shaw's first draft has, as setting, "a lady's bed-chamber"—but no locale. The characters are equally nameless labels taken from popular melodrama: the Father, the Daughter, the Heroic Lover, the Stranger. Shaw, needing a location for his war, went to Sidney Webb, his most knowledgeable friend, for help. In "two minutes," Webb came up with a suggestion. The Bulgarians had bested the Serbians in a small war in 1885. All Shaw would have to do would be to look up the *Annual Register* for that year in the British Museum Reading Room, Shaw's "university," and fill in the blanks. He set the play first in Serbia, then shifted it to Bulgaria, making, he told actor Charles Charrington, "absurd alterations in detail for the sake of local color . . . which will intensify the extravagance of the play." Shaw made his trespasser in the bedchamber an intruder of a different sort—a competent Swiss mercenary among the military amateurs. "Put a Republican—say a Swiss—into the tyrant-ridden East," Shaw said, describing his strategy, "and there you are." He thought of calling the play *Alps and Balkans,* but settled for the Virgilian resonances of *Arms and the Man,* from the first line of the *Aeneid.*

In *Arms and the Man,* Shaw employs, and often inverts, the devices of traditional nineteenth-century comic melodrama. In the rigid class structure of Victorian society, a misalliance across class lines, though absurd, was often the pivot of the plot. Its resolution created the happy ending. In the fluid class structure of an emerging nation, such a crossing of class lines has a happy logic. The Bulgaria of *Arms and the Man* represents any nation struggling toward civilized modernity. "Library" is a pretentious tag for the Petkoffs' room, which holds only a few dogeared, coffee-stained paperbacks. Raina's pride in being a Petkoff—"the richest and best known [family] in our country"—reflects the absurd vanity of Catherine, her mother: "Our position is almost historical: we can go back for twenty years."

The first act of *Arms and the Man* appears to focus on the military theme—the reality underlying the romantic dreams of martial glory. Captain Bluntschli's "professional point of view" as a soldier, he explains pragmatically to the hero-worshiping Raina, is, as every soldier knows, "to live as long as we can." He keeps chocolate creams in his cartridge case; after all, he is a Switzer. The blunt-spoken outsider's name and nationality may have been adopted from Johann Kaspar Bluntschli, a Swiss professor of law and a founder of the Institute of International Law whose autobiography, published posthumously in 1884, Shaw might have found when working in the British Museum Reading Room.

Coincidence was a staple of farce, and coincidence abounds in *Arms and the Man*. The hero whose daring exploit resulted in the unexpected capitulation of the Serbs is none other than Raina's fiancé, Sergius. Bluntschli, the stranger seeking safety in her bedroom, is the negotiator who masterminds that surrender. Major Sergius Saranoff's bravery, Raina learns, comes from his horse having run away with him, resulting in some left-handed courage. A cavalry charge, Bluntschli tells her, is "like slinging a handful of peas against a window pane: first one comes; then two or three close behind him; and then all the rest in a lump." Thinking of Sergius charging at the head of his regiment, Raina exclaims, "Yes, first One! the bravest of the brave!" "Hm!" says Bluntschli, "you should see the poor devil pulling at his horse." George Orwell, then a student too young to be in the military, saw *Arms and the Man* in 1918 in a London theater filled with soldiers fresh from the Flanders front. "At this line, the audience of simple soldiers burst into a laugh which almost lifted the roof off."

When Raina offers her hand to Bluntschli as a pledge of trust and he draws his own away explaining decorously, "I must have a wash first," Raina realizes he is "a gentleman." Her boast that people of high standing in her country "wash their hands nearly every day," prepares the audience for the satire of the second act, which extracts comic mileage from social themes—class differences that are more apparent than real, the varieties of erotic intrigue, the collision of bourgeois aspirations with local actuality.

Paul Petkoff, Raina's father, will scoff that a bath more than once a week is a "ridiculous extreme." He brags of his "library" but doubts the necessity of the modern electric bell when one can just shout for the efficient Nicola. Louka, the pert, sharp-tongued maid, derides Nicola, who hopes to become the proprietor of his own shop, for having the soul of a servant who does not know how to achieve success in service. Nicola warns her in return, "you take my advice and be respectful; . . . Thats what they like; and thats how youll make most out of them." Too rebellious to accept an underling's servility—"Youll never put the soul of a servant into me"—she employs her sexual wiles to rise beyond her station. In the late nineteenth century, whether in an emerging nation or a "civilised" one like England, for an ambitious woman there were few avenues beyond a good marriage.

In the final act, although all illusions about love, heroism, and an idealized peasantry are exploded, Shaw furnishes a series of audience-pleasing—although thoroughly ironic—happy endings. Louka, Cinderella-like, will marry her "prince," the mock-heroic Sergius. He will be freed from the strain of keeping up the "higher love," which is, for any length of time, a "very fatiguing thing." Raina, having attained maturity, will escape the stultifying atmosphere of her Balkan village to become the wife not of a nobleman but of a prosperous bourgeois— a freeborn citizen, the highest rank in Switzerland. Bluntschli, otherwise a man of reason, is exposed as "a romantic idiot." Optimistic, farcical, full of sexual energy, *Arms and the Man* is a romp in which all ends unpredictably well.

The play reflects Shaw's own state of mind at the time of writing. He wrote the role of Raina for his mistress, Florence Farr. He had other women interested in him, had achieved fame as a music critic and as drama critic, and having been requested to write a play, his fourth, to rescue the Avenue Theatre, could look forward to a career as a playwright. When Annie Horniman, the producer and associate of Florence in the venture, realized that the box office would be enhanced by casting a recognized actress in the lead, Shaw wrote to Alma Murray to coax her into playing Raina. "The lady does not swear, nor does she throttle the servant like the heroine of my other play [*Widowers' Houses*] . . . for the most part she has to be romantically beautiful or else amusing in a bearably dignified way. She is a Bulgarian, and can, I suppose, wear extraordinary things if she wished." Alma agreed to play Raina, and Florence took the role of Louka, which better fit her feisty feminism. *Arms and the Man,* for which the poster for the play read, "The Chocolate Soldier is to be seen nightly," became Shaw's first box-office success.

Raina and Louka are full of life, confident of their abilities to direct and control their destinies. Each woman exudes sexual energy and is capable of using her attractiveness to achieve her goal. Raina, surprised and intrigued when the extraordinary stranger tells her that his desire is not to bed her but merely to sleep in her bed, determines to have him. Louka, realizing that Sergius, Raina's fiancé, is physically attracted to the servant and not the mistress, uses her sexual wiles to ensnare him. Once he declares pompously, "I have had you here in my arms, and will perhaps have you there again. . . . If these hands ever touch you again, they shall touch my affianced bride," Louka knows exactly how she will entrap him. Raina must exercise more cunning and strategy to entice Bluntschli into requesting Major Petkoff's permission to wed her.

In the tradition of the play in which a stranger comes to town and changes it, Bluntschli intrudes into the life of a less developed society. Liberated from Turkish rule, Bulgaria is backward but lively, and having successfully resisted Serbian aggression, has a future more promising than its past. Even the Bulgarian servant class will seize its chances for upward mobility. A benevolent and able figure, Bluntschli assists the young nation in solving problems new to it since independence. Raina and Louka look forward in their very different ways to becoming great ladies. Once Bluntschli has helped arrange postwar demobilization, he will return for Raina, taking her with him to Switzerland. She wants Bluntschli, is relieved to be rid of Sergius, and has some measure of sophistication. Release from Bulgaria will enable her to achieve success and satisfaction. Her wit, charm, and intelligence will enable her to adjust to life as a prosperous matron. Louka's assets are her brazenness and her body, and Sergius's social position will guarantee her acceptability in an aspiring nation where rank always remains fluid.

Bluntschli is heir to a string of Swiss hotels—the ultimate in democratic gentility—the symbol of civilization and prosperity. As the owner of two hundred horses, seventy carriages, thousands of sheets, blankets, and tablecloths, more than ten thousand forks, spoons, and knives, six palatial establishments, and much more, he must be, Petkoff exclaims, "the Emperor of Switzerland." Bluntschli considers the shrewd and undervalued Nicola to be the ablest man in Bulgaria. If Nicola can speak French and German, Bluntschli will tap him to run a hotel in Switzerland. If Nicola cannot, one can imagine Bluntschli using the opportunity to add a seventh hotel to his chain, opening a hotel in Bulgaria rather than losing Nicola's skills.

In Bluntschli one can see the influence of Shaw's bookish friend and political ally Sidney Webb, who did not appear to have a molecule of romance about him. After Webb had suggested the Servo-Bulgarian War as setting for the play, Shaw consulted Sergius Stepniak, an émigré Russian artillery officer who had turned revolutionary and assassinated the head of the Russian secret police in 1878. He fled to Switzerland and then to England. Although Sergius's name suggests Stepniak, the braggart mock romantic hero seems to be a stock figure borrowed from commedia dell'arte. Knowledgeable theatergoers, however, would have recognized in Sergius the liberal politician and adventurer—and Shaw's acquaintance—Sir Robert Cunninghame Graham. Graham's memorable declarations in the House of Commons, "I never explain" and "I never withdraw," are echoed in Sergius's pompous "I never apologize." Stepniak introduced Shaw to E. A. Serebryekov, a Russian ex-naval officer before he jumped ship and escaped to England on learning he was suspected of nihilist affiliations. Serebryekov had served in the Servo-Bulgarian War as an admiral of the Bulgarian fleet on the Danube, a small flotilla. To Shaw, Serebryekov "was a magnificent figure, a tall broad-shouldered, fair-haired Russian, with mustache and flowing beard, flashing eyes, perfect teeth. As soon as I saw him, I made him my model for Sergius." Shaw also took the Russian's advice on such matters as whether a Bulgarian house might have two stories. Shaw had wanted three; Serebryekov said that was impossible as Bulgarian houses rarely had even a second story. Likewise Petkoff could not be a general or a colonel in impoverished Bulgaria but only a major—and even then not until the peace negotiations were underway.

Arms and the Man can also be seen as a coming-of-age play. Raina, although twenty-three, is emotionally much closer to the seventeen that Bluntschli thinks she is. Full of romantic ideas and still a child in her parents' house, she achieves a level of independence and maturity only hinted at in the first act. In a remarkable foreshadowing of Freudian theory, the play's sub-text can be viewed as a problem-solving dream, one that reflects upon and illuminates the manifest play.[1] In this dream, Raina must outgrow her infantile relationship to her father, reject the husband he has chosen for her, and mature enough to enter into a love relationship with the man of her choice. As if reminding us that what we are seeing is, on one level, a dream, in the confusion in the second act Shaw has Major Petkoff say of Raina, "She's dreaming, as usual." This is not the first reference to Raina's sleeping and dreaming. In the first lines of the play, Catherine says to Raina, "Louka told me you were asleep," and Raina answers her "dreamily." In Shaw's comic self-interview for *The Star*, April 14, 1894, he tells the alleged reporter, "Romantic dreams and Quixotic ideals flourish luxuriantly in the rose valleys of that country [Bulgaria]. They play their due part in 'Arms and the Man.'"

In the opening scene, now-recognizable Freudian symbols abound, from the candlesticks beside her bed to the view of the mountains through her window. Captain Bluntschli has no difficulty in climbing *up* the drainpipe to get into Raina's room, but he is terrified of going *down* that same drainpipe. Perhaps the most startling symbol is Bluntschli's exposed pistol, which has been tossed onto the ottoman in the bedroom. Although the pistol is in plain sight, neither Catherine nor the Russian officer who searches the room sees it. Nor does Raina, at first. No one does except Louka, who "sees the revolver lying on the ottoman, and stops, petrified." After the others leave the bedroom, Raina "sits on the pistol, and jumps up with a shriek." She is very disappointed to learn that the pistol is not loaded. Such symbols, which seem so obvious now, had not yet been explicated by Freud, whose *Interpretation of Dreams* would not be published in German until 1899 or translated into English until 1909.

Shaw began *Arms and the Man* in 1893, but we have no idea whether he might have been aware of the ferment in early European psychoanalysis. Freud claimed that he learned from the poets and included playwrights among the poets, but he could not have known about *Arms and the Man*. The play was not staged in Germany until 1903—and then in only two performances—and was at first prevented from being produced in Vienna, for political reasons, by the wary Austrian censors. Oscar Straus's unauthorized operetta version, *Der Tapfere Soldat,* which Shaw insisted could not use a single line of dialogue from *Arms and the Man* and had to be titled "The Chocolate Cream Soldier, a musical parody of Arms and the Man [with apologies to Mr. Bernard Shaw]" did not premiere in Vienna until 1908. Does Shaw's use of such "Freudian" symbols suggest that they are universal, or might he have begun to develop his own literary parallels to Freudianism?

There would always be a friendly rivalry between Shaw and the Irish poet W. B. Yeats, who became Florence Farr's sexual companion when Shaw began courting his future wife, Charlotte Payne-Townshend. Each man respected the other Irishman's ability and vision. Yeats's sentimental short play *The Land of Heart's Desire* was the Avenue Theatre's curtain raiser. When its companion piece, John Todhunter's *A Comedy of Sighs,* failed, Shaw rushed *Arms and the Man* to completion. Yeats, sitting through rehearsals of the work that was to rescue the production of his own play, remained unimpressed. So, he claimed, was the audience at the opening. They had a feeling that they were being toyed with slyly and even seditiously. "The whole pit and gallery," Yeats remembered, "started to laugh at the author, and then, discovering that they themselves were being laughed at, sat there not converted—their hatred was too bitter for that—but dumbfounded, while the rest of the house cheered and laughed." Failing to realize that Shaw had written a "serious farce" unlike anything he or anyone else had experienced, Yeats sat through the opening "with admiration and hatred. It seemed to me inorganic, logical straightness and not the

crooked road of life, yet I stood aghast before its energy. . . .
Presently, I had a nightmare that I was haunted by a sewing-
machine, that clicked and shone, but the incredible thing was
that the machine smiled, smiled perpetually." Yeats could not
realize that *Arms and the Man* lacked any "logical straightness" because its dreamlike structure was perhaps the opening
shot in what would become theater of the absurd.

After the first performance of *Arms and the Man* on April
21, 1894, Shaw appeared onstage for the then traditional curtain call for the author. Amid the rather timid applause, a soli-
tary "Boo!" could be heard, and Shaw facetiously responded,
"My dear fellow, I quite agree with you, but what are we two
against so many?" The audience cheered. But an unsigned review in the afternoon edition of *The Star* began, "Enormously
amusing, if slightly perplexing." Obviously something very
new to the stage had happened, as was clear when Shaw's clos-
est friend in the dramatic community, *The World*'s drama critic
William Archer, objected to the play in his review. The opportunity for "genuine fantastic comedy," he argued, vanished after the first act, replaced by "crude and contorted psychology."
Shaw, Archer complained, misunderstanding what he had seen,
had "a peculiar habit of straining all the red corpuscles out of
the blood of his personages."

A decade later the *Saturday Review* critic Max Beerbohm
wrote of a well-received revival of the play, "I am quite sure
that if I had been in the Avenue Theatre on that historic first
night I should have been very indignant against the whole affair . . . I should have heartily agreed, next morning, with the
elderly men who at the time monopolised dramatic criticism on
the daily papers, that it was a very cheap joke to represent a
soldier as shivering and whining after he had been for three
days under fire, and as being in the habit of carrying chocolates
into battle. . . . The whole play would have seemed to me a dis-
agreeable fantasy. . . . Since that time . . . I have come to see
that much of this seeming fantasy and flippance was a mere
striving after sober reality, and the reason why it appeared fantastic was that it did not conform to certain conventions of the

theatre which the majority of playgoers took as a necessary part of truth to life. . . . It is a brilliant thing, this play. . . ."

In response to the carping of those "eldery men who . . . monopolised dramatic criticism," Shaw published in *The New Review,* on July 7, 1894, "A Dramatic Realist to His Critics." There he elaborated upon "the misunderstanding between my real world and the stage world." The comedy arose, he explained, from the collision of realities with illusions, and how such encounters impact on people who must separate "stageland" from life, for when one's ideals fail to fit the facts, life cannot be fully and freely lived until the false assumptions are discarded.

By then *Arms and the Man* had run a respectable fifty performances and gone on a successful provincial tour. Writing to Sidney Webb in 1898, Shaw told him that it had "brought me in [the equivalent of] 2½ yrs Saturday [*Saturday Review*] salary from first to last (£829–11–9)" enabling him to give "the Saturday notice that I shall drop them at the end of the season." In America, it had even further success: a decent run in Chicago, and bringing in the then considerable sum of $1,000 for a single night's performance in New York. Shaw had achieved independence as a playwright.

In Berlin and Vienna the play in translation ran into censorship problems. In a 1903 letter to Siegfreid Trebitsch, the Austrian translator of Shaw's plays into German, Shaw regretted that the "accuracy of the information" provided to him by the "Russian officer who commanded the Danube fleet for the Bulgarians during the war" caused Trebitsch so much trouble with the censor. As late as 1924 the Bulgarian minister to Germany protested alleged slurs on Bulgarians and forced the producer of *Helden* (*Heroes*, the German title) to make cuts in the text. Shaw responded to the *Berliner Tageblatt* that it was "the business of the writer of a comedy to wound the susceptibilities of his audience." Such outraged sensibilities had not affected *The Chocolate Soldier*, the English version of the sentimental *Der Tapfere Soldat*, which Shaw saw reluctantly and belatedly in London in November 1910, two months after it opened. He had to stand because the house was completely sold out.

In 1930 British International Pictures had produced Shaw's *How She Lied to Her Husband* with Cecil Lewis as director, but the results were amateurish and the film quickly disappeared. In 1932 Shaw permitted them to make a second attempt at filming one of his plays, this time *Arms and the Man*. Shaw advised Cecil Lewis on new film sequences but didn't write anything new for the production. He did allow and even suggested some cuts and changes, but oversaw none of it. The film opened at Malvern in August 1932. Reviews ranged from damning it with the faintest of praise to condemnation, Allardyce Nicoll writing, "No more dismal film has ever been shown to the public." In September 1941, Shaw wrote his own scenario for Gabriel Pascal for a film version of the play. It opened with the battlefield scene in which Sergius led a cavalry charge against enemy machine guns.

> BLUNTSCHLI: Charge a battery of machine-guns! They couldn't be such damned fools. . . . Well, we shall just make holes in them, poor devils. . . . How are we off for ammunition?
>
> SERGEANT: Captain, they've sent us the wrong belts. The guns won't work.
>
> BLUNTSCHLI: Damnation! [*Peremptorily*] Run for it. Save himself who can. . . . And my revolver isn't loaded, confound it.
>
> 1ST LIEUT.: Same here.
>
> 2ND LIEUT.: Same here.

The fleeing Bluntschli purchases a loaf of bread from a peasant woman, generously paying her the price of ten loaves for the one. At a town meeting in the square, where the mayor announces the end of the war, Petkoff makes a speech in which he tells the crowd:

> [Y]ou must keep a sharp lookout for Serbian runaways. I have just heard that one of your old women has been robbed within a hundred yards of the village by a scoundrel in Serbian uniform . . . a cowardly swine sprang from the bushes, flung her brutally to the ground and trampled on her until she lost her

senses. When she recovered the fellow was gone and her basket was empty: he had not left the poor woman a single crumb. Hunt that man down.

Resisting Nazi Germany virtually alone, England was still reeling from the Blitz, the daily air raids from mid-1940 into mid-1941. It was the wrong time for a comedy that mocked war, propaganda, lies, and false heroism. The film was never produced.

In 1940 the Metro-Goldwyn-Mayer studio had failed to get Shaw's permission to film *Arms and the Man*. Shaw demanded more money than MGM wished to pay. Using the music from Straus's *Der Tapfere Soldat* and the scenario from Ferenc Molner's play *Testör*, MGM filmed an unauthorized *The Chocolate Soldier* starring Nelson Eddy and Rise Stevens, which jettisoned the satire for the romance. Shaw, for whom comedy was always a serious business, hated the film. Although nominated for three Oscars, MGM's *The Chocolate Soldier* is now forgotten.

Arms and the Man has weathered far better than its watered-down adaptations. Still as fresh as it was more than a century ago, it is rarely off the boards. It is played in a myriad of languages everywhere there are stages. Popular melodrama presented war as gloriously ennobling. For Shaw, war was non-heroic, full of paperwork, prosaic routine, and absurdity—and worse. War and love and upward mobility are still with us, and Shaw's spin on all three still resonates.

NOTE

1. For a more detailed discussion of *Arms and the Man* as a dream play, see "Oh, the Dreaming, the Dreaming," Rodelle Weintraub, *Shaw and Other Matters*, (Susquehanna University Press, Selinsgrove, PA, 1998), pp. 31–40.

Preface

Readers of the discourse with which the preceding volume commences will remember that I turned my hand to play-writing when a great deal of talk about "the New Drama," followed by the actual establishment of a "New Theatre" (the Independent), threatened to end in the humiliating discovery that the New Drama, in England at least, was a figment of the revolutionary imagination. This was not to be endured. I had rashly taken up the case; and rather than let it collapse I manufactured the evidence.

Man is a creature of habit. You cannot write three plays and then stop. Besides, the New movement did not stop. In 1894, Florence Farr, who had already produced Ibsen's Rosmersholm, was placed in command of the Avenue Theatre in London for a season on the new lines by Miss A. E. F. Horniman, who had family reasons for not yet appearing openly as a pioneer-manageress. There were, as available New Dramatists, myself, discovered by the Independent Theatre (at my own suggestion); Dr John Todhunter, who had been discovered before (his play The Black Cat had been one of the Independent's successes); and Mr W. B. Yeats, a genuine discovery. Dr Todhunter supplied A Comedy of Sighs: Mr Yeats, The Land of Heart's Desire. I, having nothing but unpleasant plays in my desk, hastily completed a first attempt at a pleasant one, and called it Arms and The Man, taking the title from the first line of Dryden's Virgil. It passed for a success, the applause on the first night being as promising as could be wished; and it ran from the 21st of April to the 7th of July. To witness it the public paid £1777:5:6, an average of

£23:2:5 per representation (including nine matinées). A publisher receiving £1700 for a book would have made a satisfactory profit: experts in West End theatrical management will contemplate that figure with a grim smile.

. . .

Returning now to the actual state of things, it is clear that I have no grievance against our theatres. Knowing quite well what I was doing, I have heaped difficulties in the way of the performance of my plays by ignoring the majority of the manager's customers: nay, by positively making war on them. To the actor I have been more considerate, using all my cunning to enable him to make the most of his technical methods; but I have not hesitated on occasion to tax his intelligence very severely, making the stage effect depend not only on *nuances* of execution quite beyond the average skill produced by the routine of the English stage in its present condition, but on a perfectly sincere and straightforward conception of states of mind which still seem cynically perverse to most people, and on a goodhumoredly contemptuous or profoundly pitiful attitude towards ethical conventions which seem to them validly heroic or venerable. It is inevitable that actors should suffer more than most of us from the sophistication of their consciousness by romance; and my view of romance as the great heresy to be swept off from art and life—as the food of modern pessimism and the bane of modern self-respect, is far more puzzling to the performers than it is to the pit. It is hard for an actor whose point of honor it is to be a perfect gentleman, to sympathize with an author who regards gentility as a dishonest folly, and gallantry and chivalry as treasonable to women and stultifying to men.

The misunderstanding is complicated by the fact that actors, in their demonstrations of emotion, have made a second nature of stage custom, which is often very much out of date as a representation of contemporary life. Sometimes the stage custom is not only obsolete, but fundamentally wrong: for instance, in the simple case of laughter and tears, in which it deals too liberally, it is certainly not based on the fact, easily enough discoverable in real life, that we only cry now in the effort to bear happiness, whilst we laugh and exult in destruction, confusion, and ruin. When a comedy is performed, it is nothing to me that the spectators laugh: any fool can make an audience laugh. I want to see how many of them, laughing or grave, are in the melting mood. And this result cannot be achieved, even by actors who thoroughly understand my purpose, except through an artistic beauty of execution unattainable without long and arduous practice, and an intellectual effort which my plays probably do not seem serious enough to call forth.

Beyond the difficulties thus raised by the nature and quality of my work, I have none to complain of. I have come upon no ill will, no inaccessibility, on the part of the very few managers with whom I have discussed it. As a rule I find that the actor-manager is over-sanguine, because he has the artist's habit of underrating the force of circumstances and exaggerating the power of the talented individual to prevail against them; whilst I have acquired the politician's habit of regarding the individual, however talented, as having no choice but to make the most of his circumstances. I half suspect that those managers who have had most to do with me, if asked to name the main obstacle to the performance of my plays, would unhesitatingly and unanimously reply "The author." And I confess that though as a matter of business I wish my plays to be performed, as a matter of instinct I fight against the inevitable misrepresentation of them with all the subtlety needed to conceal my ill will from myself as well as from the manager.

The main difficulty, of course, is the incapacity for serious drama of thousands of playgoers of all classes whose shillings and half guineas will buy as much in the market as if they delighted in the highest art. But with them I must frankly take the superior position. I know that many managers are wholly dependent on them, and that no manager is wholly independent of them; but I can no more write what they want than Joachim can put aside his fiddle and oblige a happy company of bean-feasters with a marching tune on the German concertina. They must keep away from my plays: that is all.

There is no reason, however, why I should take this haughty

attitude towards those representative critics whose complaint is that my talent, though not unentertaining, lacks elevation of sentiment and seriousness of purpose. They can find, under the surface-brilliancy for which they give me credit, no coherent thought or sympathy, and accuse me, in various terms and degrees, of an inhuman and freakish wantonness; of preoccupation with "the seamy side of life"; of paradox, cynicism, and eccentricity, reducible, as some contend, to a trite formula of treating bad as good and good as bad, important as trivial and trivial as important, serious as laughable and laughable as serious, and so forth. As to this formula I can only say that if any gentleman is simple enough to think that even a good comic opera can be produced by it, I invite him to try his hand, and see whether anything resembling one of my plays will reward him.

I could explain the matter easily enough if I chose; but the result would be that the people who misunderstand the plays would misunderstand the explanation ten times more. The particular exceptions taken are seldom more than symptoms of the underlying fundamental disagreement between the romantic morality of the critics and the natural morality of the plays. For example, I am quite aware that the much criticized Swiss officer in Arms and The Man is not a conventional stage soldier. He suffers from want of food and sleep; his nerves go to pieces after three days under fire, ending in the horrors of a rout and pursuit; he has found by experience that it is more important to have a few bits of chocolate to eat in the field than cartridges for his revolver. When many of my critics rejected these circumstances as fantastically improbable and cynically unnatural, it was not necessary to argue them into common sense: all I had to do was to brain them, so to speak, with the first half dozen military authorities at hand, beginning with the present Commander in Chief. But when it proved that such unromantic (but all the more dramatic) facts implied to them a denial of the existence of courage, patriotism, faith, hope, and charity, I saw that it was not really mere matter of fact that was at issue between us. One strongly Liberal critic, the late Moy Thomas, who had, in the teeth of a chorus of dissent, received my first

play with the most generous encouragement, declared, when
Arms and The Man was produced, that I had struck a wanton
blow at the cause of liberty in the Balkan Peninsula by men-
tioning that it was not a matter of course for a Bulgarian in
1885 to wash his hands every day. He no doubt saw soon afterwards the squabble, reported all through Europe, between
Stambouloff and an eminent lady of the Bulgarian court who
took exception to his neglect of his fingernails. After that came
the news of his ferocious assassination, with a description of
the room prepared for the reception of visitors by his widow,
who draped it with black, and decorated it with photographs
of the mutilated body of her husband. Here was a sufficiently
sensational confirmation of the accuracy of my sketch of the
theatrical nature of the first apings of western civilization by
spirited races just emerging from slavery. But it had no bearing
on the real issue between my critic and myself, which was,
whether the political and religious idealism which had inspired
Gladstone to call for the rescue of these Balkan principalities
from the despotism of the Turk, and converted miserably en-
slaved provinces into hopeful and gallant little States, will sur-
vive the general onslaught on idealism which is implicit, and
indeed explicit, in Arms and The Man and the naturalist plays
of the modern school. For my part I hope not; for idealism,
which is only a flattering name for romance in politics and
morals, is as obnoxious to me as romance in ethics or religion.
In spite of a Liberal Revolution or two, I can no longer be satisfied with fictitious morals and fictitious good conduct, shed-
ding fictitious glory on robbery, starvation, disease, crime, drink,
war, cruelty, cupidity, and all the other commonplaces of civilization which drive men to the theatre to make foolish pre-
tences that such things are progress, science, morals, religion,
patriotism, imperial supremacy, national greatness and all the
other names the newspapers call them. On the other hand, I see
plenty of good in the world working itself out as fast as the ide-
alists will allow it; and if they would only let it alone and learn
to respect reality, which would include the beneficial exercise of
respecting themselves, and incidentally respecting me, we should

all get along much better and faster. At all events, I do not see moral chaos and anarchy as the alternative to romantic convention; and I am not going to pretend I do merely to please the people who are convinced that the world is held together only by the force of unanimous, strenuous, eloquent, trumpet-tongued lying. To me the tragedy and comedy of life lie in the consequences, sometimes terrible, sometimes ludicrous, of our persistent attempts to found our institutions on the ideals suggested to our imaginations by our half-satisfied passions, instead of on a genuinely scientific natural history. And with that hint as to what I am driving at, I withdraw and ring up the curtain.

Arms and the Man

ACT I

Night: A lady's bedchamber in Bulgaria, in a small town near the Dragoman Pass, late in November in the year 1885. Through an open window with a little balcony a peak of the Balkans, wonderfully white and beautiful in the starlit snow, seems quite close at hand, though it is really miles away. The interior of the room is not like anything to be seen in the west of Europe. It is half rich Bulgarian, half cheap Viennese. Above the head of the bed, which stands against a little wall cutting off the left hand corner of the room, is a painted wooden shrine, blue and gold, with an ivory image of Christ, and a light hanging before it in a pierced metal ball suspended by three chains. The principal seat, placed towards the other side of the room and opposite the window, is a Turkish ottoman. The counterpane and hangings of the bed, the window curtains, the little carpet, and all the ornamental textile fabrics in the room are oriental and gorgeous; the paper on the walls is occidental and paltry. The washstand, against the wall on the side nearest the ottoman and window, consists of an enamelled iron basin with a pail beneath it in a painted metal frame, and a single towel on the rail at the side. The dressing table, between the bed and the window, is a common pine table, covered with a cloth of many colors, with an expensive toilet mirror on it. The door is on the side nearest the bed; and there is a chest of drawers between. This chest of drawers is also covered by a variegated native cloth; and on it there is a pile of paper backed novels, a box of chocolate creams, and a miniature easel with a large photo-

*graph of an extremely handsome officer, whose lofty bearing
and magnetic glance can be felt even from the portrait. The
room is lighted by a candle on the chest of drawers, and another on the dressing table with a box of matches beside it.*

*The window is hinged doorwise and stands wide open.
Outside, a pair of wooden shutters, opening outwards, also
stand open. On the balcony a young lady, intensely conscious of the romantic beauty of the night, and of the fact
that her own youth and beauty are part of it, is gazing at the
snowy Balkans. She is in her nightgown, well covered by a
long mantle of furs, worth, on a moderate estimate, about
three times the furniture of her room.*

*Her reverie is interrupted by her mother, Catherine
Petkoff, a woman over forty, imperiously energetic, with
magnificent black hair and eyes, who might be a very splendid specimen of the wife of a mountain farmer, but is deter-
mined to be a Viennese lady, and to that end wears a
fashionable tea gown on all occasions.*

CATHERINE [*entering hastily, full of good news*] Raina! [*She
pronounces it Rah-eena, with the stress on the ee*]. Raina!
[*She goes to the bed, expecting to find Raina there*]. Why,
where—? [*Raina looks into the room*]. Heavens, child! are
you out in the night air instead of in your bed? Youll catch
your death. Louka told me you were asleep.

RAINA [*dreamily*] I sent her away. I wanted to be alone. The
stars are so beautiful! What is the matter?

CATHERINE: Such news! There has been a battle.

RAINA [*her eyes dilating*] Ah! [*She comes eagerly to Catherine*].

CATHERINE: A great battle at Slivnitza! A victory! And it was
won by Sergius.

RAINA [*with a cry of delight*] Ah! [*They embrace rapturously*]
Oh, mother! [*Then, with sudden anxiety*] Is father safe?

CATHERINE: Of course: he sends me the news. Sergius is the
hero of the hour, the idol of the regiment.

RAINA: Tell me, tell me. How was it? [*Ecstatically*] Oh, mother!

mother! mother! [*She pulls her mother down on the otto-man; and they kiss one another frantically*].

CATHERINE [*with surging enthusiasm*] You cant guess how splendid it is. A cavalry charge! think of that! He defied our Russian commanders—acted without orders—led a charge on his own responsibility—headed it himself—was the first man to sweep through their guns. Cant you see it, Raina: our gallant splendid Bulgarians with their swords and eyes flashing, thundering down like an avalanche and scattering the wretched Serbs and their dandified Austrian officers like chaff. And you! you kept Sergius waiting a year before you would be betrothed to him. Oh, if you have a drop of Bulgarian blood in your veins, you will worship him when he comes back.

RAINA: What will he care for my poor little worship after the acclamations of a whole army of heroes? But no matter: I am so happy! so proud! [*She rises and walks about excitedly*]. It proves that all our ideas were real after all.

CATHERINE [*indignantly*] Our ideas real! What do you mean?

RAINA: Our ideas of what Sergius would do. Our patriotism. Our heroic ideals. I sometimes used to doubt whether they were anything but dreams. Oh, what faithless little creatures girls are! When I buckled on Sergius's sword he looked so noble: it was treason to think of disillusion or humiliation or failure. And yet—and yet—[*She sits down again suddenly*] Promise me youll never tell him.

CATHERINE: Dont ask me for promises until I know what I'm promising.

RAINA: Well, it came into my head just as he was holding me in his arms and looking into my eyes, that perhaps we only had our heroic ideas because we are so fond of reading Byron and Pushkin, and because we were so delighted with the opera that season at Bucharest. Real life is so seldom like that! indeed never, as far as I knew it then. [*Remorsefully*] Only think, mother: I doubted him: I wondered whether all his heroic qualities and his soldiership might not prove mere imagination when he went into a real battle. I had an uneasy fear that he might cut a poor figure there beside all those clever officers from the Tsar's court.

CATHERINE: A poor figure! Shame on you! The Serbs have Austrian officers who are just as clever as the Russians; but we have beaten them in every battle for all that.

RAINA [*laughing and snuggling against her mother*] Yes: I was only a prosaic little coward. Oh, to think that it was all true! that Sergius is just as splendid and noble as he looks! that the world is really a glorious world for women who can see its glory and men who can act its romance! What happiness! what unspeakable fulfilment!

They are interrupted by the entry of Louka, a handsome proud girl in a pretty Bulgarian peasant's dress with double apron, so defiant that her servility to Raina is almost insolent. She is afraid of Catherine, but even with her goes as far as she dares.

LOUKA: If you please, madam, all the windows are to be closed and the shutters made fast. They say there may be shooting in the streets. [*Raina and Catherine rise together, alarmed*]. The Serbs are being chased right back through the pass; and they say they may run into the town. Our cavalry will be after them; and our people will be ready for them, you may be sure, now theyre running away. [*She goes out on the balcony, and pulls the outside shutters to; then steps back into the room*].

CATHERINE [*businesslike, housekeeping instincts aroused*] I must see that everything is made safe downstairs.

RAINA: I wish our people were not so cruel. What glory is there in killing wretched fugitives?

CATHERINE: Cruel! Do you suppose they would hesitate to kill you—or worse?

RAINA [*to Louka*] Leave the shutters so that I can just close them if I hear any noise.

CATHERINE [*authoritatively, turning on her way to the door*] Oh no, dear: you must keep them fastened. You would be sure to drop off to sleep and leave them open. Make them fast, Louka.

LOUKA: Yes, madam. [*She fastens them*].

RAINA: Dont be anxious about me. The moment I hear a shot, I shall blow out the candles and roll myself up in bed with my ears well covered.

CATHERINE: Quite the wisest thing you can do, my love. Goodnight.

RAINA: Goodnight. [*Her emotion comes back for a moment*]. Wish me joy [*They kiss*]. This is the happiest night of my life—if only there are no fugitives.

CATHERINE: Go to bed, dear; and dont think of them. [*She goes out*].

LOUKA [*secretly to Raina*] If you would like the shutters open, just give them a push like this [*she pushes them: they open: she pulls them to again*]. One of them ought to be bolted at the bottom; but the bolt's gone.

RAINA [*with dignity, reproving her*] Thanks, Louka; but we must do what we are told. [*Louka makes a grimace*]. Goodnight.

LOUKA [*carelessly*] Goodnight. [*She goes out, swaggering*].

Raina, left alone, takes off her fur cloak and throws it on the ottoman. Then she goes to the chest of drawers, and adores the portrait there with feelings that are beyond all expression. She does not kiss it or press it to her breast, or shew it any mark of bodily affection; but she takes it in her hands and elevates it, like a priestess.

RAINA [*looking up at the picture*] Oh, I shall never be unworthy of you any more, my soul's hero: never, never, never. [*She replaces it reverently. Then she selects a novel from the little pile of books. She turns over the leaves dreamily; finds her page; turns the book inside out at it; and, with a happy sigh, gets into bed and prepares to read herself to sleep. But before abandoning herself to fiction, she raises her eyes once more, thinking of the blessed reality, and murmurs*] My hero! my hero!

A distant shot breaks the quiet of the night. She starts, listening; and two more shots, much nearer, follow, startling her so that she scrambles out of bed, and hastily blows out the candle on the chest of drawers. Then, putting her fingers in her ears, she runs to the dressing table, blows out the light there, and hurries back to bed in the dark, nothing being visible but the glimmer of the light in the pierced ball before the image, and the starlight seen through the slits at the top of the shutters. The firing breaks out again: there is a startling fusillade quite close at hand. Whilst it is still echoing, the shutters disappear, pulled open from without; and for an instant the rectangle of snowy starlight flashes out with the figure of a man silhouetted in black upon it. The shutters close immediately; and the room is dark again. But the silence is now broken by the sound of panting. Then there is a scratch; and the flame of a match is seen in the middle of the room.

RAINA [*crouching on the bed*] Who's there? [*The match is out instantly*]. Who's there? Who is that?

A MAN'S VOICE [*in the darkness, subduedly, but threateningly*] Sh—sh! Dont call out; or youll be shot. Be good; and no harm will happen to you. [*She is heard leaving her bed, and making for the door*]. Take care: it's no use trying to run away.

RAINA: But who—

THE VOICE [*warning*] Remember: if you raise your voice my revolver will go off. [*Commandingly*]. Strike a light and let me see you. Do you hear. [*Another moment of silence and darkness as she retreats to the chest of drawers. Then she lights a candle; and the mystery is at an end. He is a man of about 35, in a deplorable plight, bespattered with mud and blood and snow, his belt and the strap of his revolver-case keeping together the torn ruins of the blue tunic of a Serbian artillery officer. All that the candlelight and his unwashed unkempt condition make it possible to discern is that he is of middling stature and undistinguished appearance, with strong neck and shoulders, roundish obstinate looking head covered with short crisp bronze curls, clear quick eyes and good brows and mouth, hopelessly prosaic nose like that of a strong minded baby, trim soldierlike carriage and energetic manner, and with all his wits about him in spite of his des-*

perate predicament: even with a sense of the humor of it, without, however, the least intention of trifling with it or throwing away a chance. Reckoning up what he can guess about Raina: her age, her social position, her character, and the extent to which she is frightened, he continues, more politely but still most determinedly] Excuse my disturbing you; but you recognize my uniform? Serb! If I'm caught I shall be killed. *[Menacingly]* Do you understand that?

RAINA: Yes.

THE MAN: Well, I don't intend to get killed if I can help it. *[Still more formidably]* Do you understand that? *[He locks the door quickly but quietly]*.

RAINA: *[disdainfully]* I suppose not. *[She draws herself up superbly, and looks him straight in the face, adding, with cutting emphasis]* Some soldiers, I know, are afraid to die.

THE MAN *[with grim goodhumor]* All of them, dear lady, all of them, believe me. It is our duty to live as long as we can. Now, if you raise an alarm—

RAINA *[cutting him short]* You will shoot me. How do you know that *I* am afraid to die?

THE MAN *[cunningly]* Ah; but suppose I dont shoot you, what will happen then? A lot of your cavalry will burst into this pretty room of yours and slaughter me here like a pig; for I'll fight like a demon: they shant get me into the street to amuse themselves with: I know what they are. Are you prepared to receive that sort of company in your present undress? *[Raina, suddenly conscious of her nightgown, instinctively shrinks and gathers it more closely about her neck. He watches her and adds pitilessly]* Hardly presentable, eh? *[She turns to the ottoman. He raises his pistol instantly, and cries]* Stop! *[She stops]*. Where are you going?

RAINA *[with dignified patience]* Only to get my cloak.

THE MAN *[passing swiftly to the ottoman and snatching the cloak]* A good idea! I'll keep the cloak; and youll take care that nobody comes in and sees you without it. This is a better weapon than the revolver: eh? *[He throws the pistol down on the ottoman]*.

RAINA [*revolted*] It is not the weapon of a gentleman!

THE MAN: It's good enough for a man with only you to stand between him and death. [*As they look at one another for a moment, Raina hardly able to believe that even a Serbian officer can be so cynically and selfishly unchivalrous, they are startled by a sharp fusillade in the street. The chill of imminent death hushes the man's voice as he adds*] Do you hear? If you are going to bring those blackguards in on me you shall receive them as you are.

    Clamor and disturbance. The pursuers in the street batter at the house door, shouting Open the door! Open the door! Wake up, will you! *A man servant's voice calls to them angrily from within* This is Major Petkoff's house: you cant come in here; *but a renewal of the clamor, and a torrent of blows on the door, end with his letting a chain down with a clank, followed by a rush of heavy footsteps and a din of triumphant yells, dominated at last by the voice of Catherine, indignantly addressing an officer with* What does this mean, sir? Do you know where you are? *The noise subsides suddenly.*

LOUKA [*outside, knocking at the bedroom door*] My lady! my lady! get up quick and open the door. If you dont they will break it down.

    The fugitive throws up his head with the gesture of a man who sees that it is all over with him, and drops the manner he has been assuming to intimidate Raina.

THE MAN [*sincerely and kindly*] No use, dear: I'm done for. [*Flinging the cloak to her*] Quick! wrap yourself up: they're coming.

RAINA: Oh, thank you. [*She wraps herself up with intense relief*].

THE MAN [*between his teeth*] Dont mention it.

RAINA [*anxiously*] What will you do?

THE MAN [*grimly*] The first man in will find out. Keep out of the way; and dont look. It wont last long; but it will not be nice. [*He draws his sabre and faces the door, waiting*].

RAINA [*impulsively*] I'll help you. I'll save you.

THE MAN: You cant.

RAINA: I can. I'll hide you. [*She drags him towards the window*]. Here! behind the curtains.

THE MAN [*yielding to her*] Theres just half a chance, if you keep your head.

RAINA [*drawing the curtain before him*] S-sh! [*She makes for the ottoman*].

THE MAN [*putting out his head*] Remember—

RAINA [*running back to him*] Yes?

THE MAN: —nine soldiers out of ten are born fools.

RAINA: Oh! [*She draws the curtain angrily before him*].

THE MAN [*looking out at the other side*] If they find me, I promise you a fight: a devil of a fight.

   She stamps at him. He disappears hastily. She takes off her cloak, and throws it across the foot of the bed. Then, with a sleepy, disturbed air, she opens the door. Louka enters excitedly.

LOUKA: One of those beasts of Serbs has been seen climbing up the waterpipe to your balcony. Our men want to search for him; and they are so wild and drunk and furious. [*She makes for the other side of the room to get as far from the door as possible*]. My lady says you are to dress at once and to—[*She sees the revolver lying on the ottoman, and stops, petrified*].

RAINA [*as if annoyed at being disturbed*] They shall not search here. Why have they been let in?

CATHERINE [*coming in hastily*] Raina, darling, are you safe? Have you seen anyone or heard anything?

RAINA: I heard the shooting. Surely the soldiers will not dare come in here?

CATHERINE: I have found a Russian officer, thank Heaven: he knows Sergius. [*Speaking through the door to someone outside*] Sir: will you come in now. My daughter will receive you.

   A young Russian officer, in Bulgarian uniform, enters, sword in hand.

OFFICER [*with soft feline politeness and stiff military carriage*] Good evening, gracious lady. I am sorry to intrude; but there is a Serb hiding on the balcony. Will you and the gracious lady your mother please to withdraw whilst we search?

RAINA [*petulantly*] Nonsense, sir: you can see that there is no one on the balcony. [*She throws the shutters wide open and stands with her back to the curtain where the man is hidden, pointing to the moonlit balcony. A couple of shots are fired right under the window; and a bullet shatters the glass opposite Raina, who winks and gasps, but stands her ground; whilst Catherine screams, and the officer, with a cry of* Take care! *rushes to the balcony*].

THE OFFICER [*on the balcony, shouting savagely down to the street*] Cease firing there, you fools: do you hear? Cease firing, damn you! [*He glares down for a moment; then turns to Raina, trying to resume his polite manner*]. Could anyone have got in without your knowledge? Were you asleep?

RAINA: No: I have not been to bed.

THE OFFICER [*impatiently, coming back into the room*] Your neighbors have their heads so full of runaway Serbs that they see them everywhere. [*Politely*] Gracious lady: a thousand pardons. Goodnight. [*Military bow, which Raina returns coldly. Another to Catherine, who follows him out*].

Raina closes the shutters. She turns and sees Louka, who has been watching the scene curiously.

RAINA: Dont leave my mother, Louka, until the soldiers go away.

Louka glances at Raina, at the ottoman, at the curtain; then purses her lips secretively, laughs insolently, and goes out. Raina, highly offended by this demonstration, follows her to the door, and shuts it behind her with a slam, locking it violently. The man immediately steps out from behind the curtain, sheathing his sabre. Then, dismissing the danger from his mind in a businesslike way, he comes affably to Raina.

THE MAN: A narrow shave; but a miss is as good as a mile. Dear young lady: your servant to the death. I wish for your sake I had joined the Bulgarian army instead of the other one. I am not a native Serb.

RAINA [*haughtily*] No: you are one of the Austrians who set the Serbs on to rob us of our national liberty, and who officer their army for them. We hate them!

THE MAN: Austrian! not I. Dont hate me, dear young lady. I am a Swiss, fighting merely as a professional soldier. I joined the Serbs because they came first on the road from Switzerland. Be generous: youve beaten us hollow.

RAINA: Have I not been generous?

THE MAN: Noble! Heroic! But I'm not saved yet. This particular rush will soon pass through; but the pursuit will go on all night by fits and starts. I must take my chance to get off in a quiet interval. [*Pleasantly*] You dont mind my waiting just a minute or two, do you?

RAINA [*putting on her most genteel society manner*] Oh, not at all. Wont you sit down?

THE MAN: Thanks [*He sits on the foot of the bed*].

   Raina walks with studied elegance to the ottoman and sits down. Unfortunately she sits on the pistol, and jumps up with a shriek. The man, all nerves, shies like a frightened horse to the other side of the room.

THE MAN [*irritably*] Dont frighten me like that. What is it?

RAINA: Your revolver! It was staring that officer in the face all the time. What an escape!

THE MAN [*vexed at being unnecessarily terrified*] Oh, is that all?

RAINA [*staring at him rather superciliously as she conceives a poorer and poorer opinion of him, and feels proportionately more and more at her ease*] I am sorry I frightened you. [*She takes up the pistol and hands it to him*]. Pray take it to protect yourself against me.

THE MAN [*grinning wearily at the sarcasm as he takes the pistol*] No use, dear young lady: theres nothing in it. It's not loaded. [*He makes a grimace at it, and drops it disparingly into his revolver case*].

RAINA: Load it by all means.

THE MAN: Ive no ammunition. What use are cartridges in battle? I always carry chocolate instead; and I finished the last cake of that hours ago.

RAINA [*outraged in her most cherished ideals of manhood*] Chocolate! Do you stuff your pockets with sweets—like a schoolboy—even in the field?

THE MAN [*grinning*] Yes: isnt it contemptible? [*Hungrily*] I wish I had some now.

RAINA: Allow me. [*She sails away scornfully to the chest of drawers, and returns with the box of confectionery in her hand*]. I am sorry I have eaten them all except these. [*She offers him the box*].

THE MAN [*ravenously*] Youre an angel! [*He gobbles the contents*]. Creams! Delicious! [*He looks anxiously to see whether there are any more. There are none: he can only scrape the box with his fingers and suck them. When that nourishment is exhausted he accepts the inevitable with pathetic good-humor, and says, with grateful emotion*] Bless you, dear lady! You can always tell an old soldier by the inside of his holsters and cartridge boxes. The young ones carry pistols and cartridges: the old ones, grub. Thank you. [*He hands back the box. She snatches it contemptuously from him and throws it away. He shies again, as if she had meant to strike him*]. Ugh! Dont do things so suddenly, gracious lady. It's mean to revenge yourself because I frightened you just now.

RAINA [*loftily*] Frighten me! Do you know, sir, that though I am only a woman, I think I am at heart as brave as you.

THE MAN: I should think so. You havnt been under fire for three days as I have. I can stand two days without shewing it much; but no man can stand three days: I'm as nervous as a mouse. [*He sits down on the ottoman, and takes his head in his hands*]. Would you like to see me cry?

RAINA [*alarmed*] No.

THE MAN: If you would, all you have to do is to scold me just as if I were a little boy and you my nurse. If I were in camp now, theyd play all sorts of tricks on me.

RAINA [*a little moved*] I'm sorry. I wont scold you. [*Touched by the sympathy in her tone, he raises his head and looks gratefully at her: she immediately draws back and says stiffly*] You must excuse me: our soldiers are not like that. [*She moves away from the ottoman*].

THE MAN: Oh yes they are. There are only two sorts of soldiers: old ones and young ones. I've served fourteen years: half of your fellows never smelt powder before. Why, how is it that youve just beaten us? Sheer ignorance of the art of war, nothing else. [*Indignantly*] I never saw anything so unprofessional.

RAINA [*ironically*] Oh! was it unprofessional to beat you?

THE MAN: Well, come! is it professional to throw a regiment of cavalry on a battery of machine guns, with the dead certainty that if the guns go off not a horse or man will ever get within fifty yards of the fire? I couldnt believe my eyes when I saw it.

RAINA [*eagerly turning to him, as all her enthusiasm and her dreams of glory rush back on her*] Did you see the great cavalry charge? Oh, tell me about it. Describe it to me.

THE MAN: You never saw a cavalry charge, did you?

RAINA: How could I?

THE MAN: Ah, perhaps not. No: of course not! Well, it's a funny sight. It's like slinging a handful of peas against a window pane: first one comes; then two or three close behind him; and then all the rest in a lump.

RAINA [*her eyes dilating as she raises her clasped hands ecstatically*] Yes, first One! the bravest of the brave!

THE MAN [*prosaically*] Hm! you should see the poor devil pulling at his horse.

RAINA: Why should he pull at his horse?

THE MAN [*impatient of so stupid a question*] It's running away with him, of course: do you suppose the fellow wants to get there before the others and be killed? Then they all come. You can tell the young ones by their wildness and their slashing. The old ones come bunched up under the number one guard: they know that theyre mere projectiles, and that it's no use trying to fight. The wounds are mostly broken knees, from the horses cannoning together.

RAINA: Ugh! But I dont believe the first man is a coward. I know he is a hero!

THE MAN [*goodhumoredly*] Thats what youd have said if youd seen the first man in the charge today.

RAINA [*breathless, forgiving him everything*] Ah, I knew it! Tell me. Tell me about him.

THE MAN: He did it like an operatic tenor. A regular handsome fellow, with flashing eyes and lovely moustache, shouting his war-cry and charging like Don Quixote at the windmills. We did laugh.

RAINA: You dared to laugh!

THE MAN: Yes; but when the sergeant ran up as white as a sheet, and told us theyd sent us the wrong ammunition, and that we couldnt fire a round for the next ten minutes, we laughed at the other side of our mouths. I never felt so sick in my life; though Ive been in one or two very tight places. And I hadnt even a revolver cartridge: only chocolate. We'd no bayonets: nothing. Of course, they just cut us to bits. And there was Don Quixote flourishing like a drum major, thinking he'd done the cleverest thing ever known, whereas he ought to be courtmartialled for it. Of all the fools ever let loose on a field of battle, that man must be the very maddest. He and his regiment simply committed suicide; only the pistol missed fire: thats all.

RAINA [*deeply wounded, but steadfastly loyal to her ideals*] Indeed! Would you know him again if you saw him?

THE MAN: Shall I ever forget him!

   She again goes to the chest of drawers. He watches her with a vague hope that she may have something more for him to eat. She takes the portrait from its stand and brings it to him.

RAINA: That is a photograph of the gentleman—the patriot and hero—to whom I am betrothed.

THE MAN [*recognizing it with a shock*] I'm really very sorry. [*Looking at her*] Was it fair to lead me on? [*He looks at the portrait again*] Yes: thats Don Quixote: not a doubt of it. [*He stifles a laugh*].

RAINA [*quickly*] Why do you laugh?

THE MAN [*apologetic, but still greatly tickled*] I didnt laugh, I assure you. At least I didnt mean to. But when I think of him charging the windmills and imagining he was doing the finest thing—[*He chokes with suppressed laughter*].

RAINA [*sternly*] Give me back the portrait, sir.

THE MAN [*with sincere remorse*] Of course. Certainly. I'm

really very sorry. [*He hands her the picture. She deliberately kisses it and looks him straight in the face before returning to the chest of drawers to replace it. He follows her, apologizing*]. Perhaps I'm quite wrong, you know: no doubt I am. Most likely he had got wind of the cartridge business somehow, and knew it was a safe job.

RAINA: That is to say, he was a pretender and a coward! You did not dare say that before.

THE MAN [*with a comic gesture of despair*] It's no use, dear lady: I cant make you see it from the professional point of view. [*As he turns away to get back to the ottoman, a couple of distant shots threaten renewed trouble*].

RAINA [*sternly, as she sees him listening to the shots*] So much the better for you!

THE MAN [*turning*] How?

RAINA: You are my enemy; and you are at my mercy. What would I do if I were a professional soldier?

THE MAN: Ah, true, dear young lady: youre always right. I know how good youve been to me: to my last hour I shall remember those three chocolate creams. It was unsoldierly; but it was angelic.

RAINA [*coldly*] Thank you. And now I will do a soldierly thing. You cannot stay here after what you have just said about my future husband; but I will go out on the balcony and see whether it is safe for you to climb down into the street. [*She turns to the window*].

THE MAN [*changing countenance*] Down that waterpipe! Stop! Wait! I cant! I darent! The very thought of it makes me giddy. I came up it fast enough with death behind me. But to face it now in cold blood—! [*He sinks on the ottoman*]. It's no use: I give up: I'm beaten. Give the alarm. [*He drops his head on his hands in the deepest dejection*].

RAINA [*disarmed by pity*] Come: dont be disheartened. [*She stoops over him almost maternally: he shakes his head*]. Oh, you are a very poor soldier: a chocolate cream soldier! Come, cheer up! it takes less courage to climb down than to face capture: remember that.

THE MAN [*dreamily, lulled by her voice*] No: capture only means death; and death is sleep: oh, sleep, sleep, sleep, undisturbed sleep! Climbing down the pipe means doing something—exerting myself—thinking! Death ten times over first.

RAINA [*softly and wonderingly, catching the rhythm of his weariness*] Are you as sleepy as that?

THE MAN: Ive not had two hours undisturbed sleep since I joined. I havnt closed my eyes for forty-eight hours.

RAINA [*at her wit's end*] But what am I to do with you?

THE MAN [*staggering up, roused by her desperation*] Of course. I must do something. [*He shakes himself; pulls himself together; and speaks with rallied vigor and courage*]. You see, sleep or no sleep, hunger or no hunger, tired or not tired, you can always do a thing when you know it must be done. Well, that pipe must be got down: [*he hits himself on the chest*] do you hear that, you chocolate cream soldier? [*He turns to the window*].

RAINA [*anxiously*] But if you fall?

THE MAN: I shall sleep as if the stones were a feather bed. Goodbye. [*He makes boldly for the window; and his hand is on the shutter when there is a terrible burst of firing in the street beneath*].

RAINA [*rushing to him*] Stop! [*She seizes him recklessly, and pulls him quite round*]. Theyll kill you.

THE MAN [*coolly, but attentively*] Never mind: this sort of thing is all in my day's work. I'm bound to take my chance. [*Decisively*] Now do what I tell you. Put out the candle; so that they shant see the light when I open the shutters. And keep away from the window, whatever you do. If they see me theyre sure to have a shot at me.

RAINA [*clinging to him*] Theyre sure to see you: it's bright moonlight. I'll save you. Oh, how can you be so indifferent! You want me to save you, dont you?

THE MAN: I really dont want to be troublesome. [*She shakes him in her impatience*]. I am not indifferent, dear young lady, I assure you. But how is it to be done?

RAINA: Come away from the window. [*She takes him firmly*

back to the middle of the room. The moment she releases him he turns mechanically towards the window again. She seizes him and turns him back, exclaiming] Please! [*He becomes motionless, like a hypnotized rabbit, his fatigue gaining fast on him. She releases him, and addresses him patronizingly*]. Now listen. You must trust to our hospitality. You do not yet know in whose house you are. I am a Petkoff.

THE MAN: A pet what?

RAINA [*rather indignantly*] I mean that I belong to the family of the Petkoffs, the richest and best known in our country.

THE MAN: Oh yes, of course. I beg your pardon. The Petkoffs, to be sure. How stupid of me!

RAINA: You know you never heard of them until this moment. How can you stoop to pretend!

THE MAN: Forgive me: I'm too tired to think; and the change of subject was too much for me. Dont scold me.

RAINA: I forgot. It might make you cry. [*He nods, quite seriously. She pouts and then resumes her patronizing tone*]. I must tell you that my father holds the highest command of any Bulgarian in our army. He is [*proudly*] a Major.

THE MAN [*pretending to be deeply impressed*] A Major! Bless me! Think of that!

RAINA: You shewed great ignorance in thinking that it was necessary to climb up to the balcony because ours is the only private house that has two rows of windows. There is a flight of stairs inside to get up and down by.

THE MAN: Stairs! How grand! You live in great luxury indeed, dear young lady.

RAINA: Do you know what a library is?

THE MAN: A library? A roomful of books?

RAINA: Yes. We have one, the only one in Bulgaria.

THE MAN: Actually a real library! I should like to see that.

RAINA [*affectedly*] I tell you these things to shew you that you are not in the house of ignorant country folk who would kill you the moment they saw your Serbian uniform, but among civilized people. We go to Bucharest every year for the opera season; and I have spent a whole month in Vienna.

THE MAN: I saw that, dear young lady. I saw at once that you knew the world.

RAINA: Have you ever seen the opera of Ernani?

THE MAN: Is that the one with the devil in it in red velvet, and a soldiers' chorus?

RAINA [*contemptuously*] No!

THE MAN [*stifling a heavy sigh of weariness*] Then I dont know it.

RAINA: I thought you might have remembered the great scene where Ernani, flying from his foes just as you are tonight, takes refuge in the castle of his bitterest enemy, an old Castilian noble. The noble refuses to give him up. His guest is sacred to him.

THE MAN [*quickly, waking up a little*] Have your people got that notion?

RAINA [*with dignity*] My mother and I can understand that notion, as you call it. And if instead of threatening me with your pistol as you did you had simply thrown yourself as a fugitive on our hospitality, you would have been as safe as in your father's house.

THE MAN: Quite sure?

RAINA [*turning her back on him in disgust*] Oh, it is useless to try to make you understand.

THE MAN: Dont be angry: you see how awkward it would be for me if there was any mistake. My father is a very hospitable man: he keeps six hotels; but I couldnt trust him as far as that. What about your father?

RAINA: He is away at Slivnitza fighting for his country. I answer for your safety. There is my hand in pledge of it. Will that reassure you? [*She offers him her hand*].

THE MAN [*looking dubiously at his own hand*] Better not touch my hand, dear young lady. I must have a wash first.

RAINA [*touched*] That is very nice of you. I see that you are a gentleman.

THE MAN [*puzzled*] Eh?

RAINA: You must not think I am surprised. Bulgarians of really good standing—people in our position—wash their hands nearly every day. So you see I can appreciate your delicacy. You may take my hand. [*She offers it again*].

THE MAN [*kissing it with his hands behind his back*] Thanks, gracious young lady: I feel safe at last. And now would you mind breaking the news to your mother? I had better not stay here secretly longer than is necessary.

RAINA: If you will be so good as to keep perfectly still whilst I am away.

THE MAN: Certainly. [*He sits down on the ottoman*].

Raina goes to the bed and wraps herself in the fur cloak. His eyes close. She goes to the door. Turning for a last look at him, she sees that he is dropping off to sleep.

RAINA [*at the door*] You are not going asleep, are you? [*He murmurs inarticulately: she runs to him and shakes him*]. Do you hear? Wake up: you are falling asleep.

THE MAN: Eh? Falling aslee—? Oh no: not the least in the world: I was only thinking. It's all right: I'm wide awake.

RAINA [*severely*] Will you please stand up while I am away. [*He rises reluctantly*]. All the time, mind.

THE MAN [*standing unsteadily*] Certainly. Certainly: you may depend on me.

Raina looks doubtfully at him. He smiles weakly. She goes reluctantly, turning again at the door, and almost catching him in the act of yawning. She goes out.

THE MAN [*drowsily*] Sleep, sleep, sleep, sleep, slee—[*The words trail off into a murmur. He wakes again with a shock on the point of falling*]. Where am I? Thats what I want to know: where am I? Must keep awake. Nothing keeps me awake except danger: remember that: [*intently*] danger, danger, danger, dan—[*trailing off again: another shock*] Wheres danger? Mus' find it. [*He starts off vaguely round the room in search of it*]. What am I looking for? Sleep—danger—dont know. [*He stumbles against the bed*]. Ah yes: now I know. All right now. I'm to go to bed, but not to sleep. Be sure not to sleep, because of danger. Not to lie down either, only sit down. [*He sits on the bed. A blissful expression comes into his face*]. Ah! [*With a happy sigh he sinks back at full length; lifts his boots*

into the bed with a final effort; and falls fast asleep instantly].
Catherine comes in, followed by Raina.

RAINA [*looking at the ottoman*] He's gone! I left him here.

CATHERINE: Here! Then he must have climbed down from the—

RAINA [*seeing him*] Oh! [*She points*].

CATHERINE [*scandalized*] Well! [*She strides to the bed, Raina following until she is opposite her on the other side*]. He's fast asleep. The brute!

RAINA [*anxiously*] Sh!

CATHERINE [*shaking him*] Sir! [*Shaking him again, harder*] Sir!! [*Vehemently, shaking very hard*] Sir!!!

RAINA [*catching her arm*] Dont, mamma; the poor darling is worn out. Let him sleep.

CATHERINE [*letting him go, and turning amazed to Raina*] The poor darling! Raina!!! [*She looks sternly at her daughter*].
The man sleeps profoundly.

ACT II

The sixth of March, 1886. In the garden of Major Petkoff's house. It is a fine spring morning: the garden looks fresh and pretty. Beyond the paling the tops of a couple of minarets can be seen, shewing that there is a valley there, with the little town in it. A few miles further the Balkan mountains rise and shut in the landscape. Looking towards them from within the garden, the side of the house is seen on the left, with a garden door reached by a little flight of steps. On the right the stable yard, with its gateway, encroaches on the garden. There are fruit bushes along the paling and house, covered with washing spread out to dry. A path runs by the house, and rises by two steps at the corner, where it turns out of sight. In the middle, a small table, with two bent wood chairs at it, is laid for breakfast with Turkish coffee pot, cups, rolls, etc.; but the cups have been used and the bread broken. There is a wooden garden seat against the wall on the right.

Louka, smoking a cigaret, is standing between the table and the house, turning her back with angry disdain on a man servant who is lecturing her. He is a middle-aged man of cool temperament and low but clear and keen intelligence, with the complacency of the servant who values himself on his rank in servitude, and the imperturbability of the accurate calculator who has no illusions. He wears a white Bulgarian costume: jacket with embroidered border, sash, wide knickerbockers, and decorated gaiters. His head is shaved up to the crown, giving him a high Japanese forehead. His name is Nicola.

NICOLA: Be warned in time, Louka: mend your manners. I know the mistress. She is so grand that she never dreams that any servant could dare be disrespectful to her; but if she once suspects that you are defying her, out you go.

LOUKA: I do defy her. I will defy her. What do I care for her?

NICOLA: If you quarrel with the family, I never can marry you. It's the same as if you quarrelled with me!

LOUKA: You take her part against me, do you?

NICOLA [sedately] I shall always be dependent on the good will of the family. When I leave their service and start a shop in Sofia, their custom will be half my capital: their bad word would ruin me.

LOUKA: You have no spirit. I should like to catch them saying a word against me!

NICOLA [pityingly] I should have expected more sense from you, Louka. But youre young: youre young!

LOUKA: Yes; and you like me the better for it, dont you? But I know some family secrets they wouldnt care to have told, young as I am. Let them quarrel with me if they dare!

NICOLA [with compassionate superiority] Do you know what they would do if they heard you talk like that?

LOUKA: What could they do?

NICOLA: Discharge you for untruthfulness. Who would believe any stories you told after that? Who would give you another situation? Who in this house would dare be seen speaking to you ever again? How long would your father be left on his little farm? [She impatiently throws away the end of her cigaret, and stamps on it]. Child: you dont know the power such high people have over the like of you and me when we try to rise out of our poverty against them. [He goes close to her and lowers his voice]. Look at me, ten years in their service. Do you think I know no secrets? I know things about the mistress that she woudnt have the master know for a thousand levas. I know things about him that she wouldnt let him hear the last of for six months if I blabbed them to her. I know things about Raina that would break off her match with Sergius if—

LOUKA [*turning on him quickly*] How do you know? I never told you!

NICOLA [*opening his eyes cunningly*] So thats your little secret, is it? I thought it might be something like that. Well, you take my advice and be respectful; and make the mistress feel that no matter what you know or dont know, she can depend on you to hold your tongue and serve the family faithfully. Thats what they like; and thats how youll make most out of them.

LOUKA [*with searching scorn*] You have the soul of a servant, Nicola.

NICOLA [*complacently*] Yes: thats the secret of success in service.

   A loud knocking with a whip handle on a wooden door is heard from the stable yard.

MALE VOICE OUTSIDE: Hollo! Hollo there! Nicola!

LOUKA: Master! back from the war!

NICOLA [*quickly*] My word for it, Louka, the war's over. Off with you and get some fresh coffee. [*He runs out into the stable yard*].

LOUKA [*as she collects the coffee pot and cups on the tray, and carries it into the house*] Youll never put the soul of a servant into me.

   Major Petkoff comes from the stable yard, followed by Nicola. He is a cheerful, excitable, insignificant, unpolished man of about 50, naturally unambitious except as to his income and his importance in local society, but just now greatly pleased with the military rank which the war has thrust on him as a man of consequence in his town. The fever of plucky patriotism which the Serbian attack roused in all the Bulgarians has pulled him through the war; but he is obviously glad to be home again.

PETKOFF [*pointing to the table with his whip*] Breakfast out here, eh?

NICOLA: Yes, sir. The mistress and Miss Raina have just gone in.

PETKOFF [*sitting down and taking a roll*] Go in and say Ive come; and get me some fresh coffee.

NICOLA: It's coming, sir. [*He goes to the house door. Louka, with fresh coffee, a clean cup, and a brandy bottle on her tray, meets him*]. Have you told the mistress?

LOUKA: Yes: she's coming.

Nicola goes into the house. Louka brings the coffee to the table.

PETKOFF: Well: the Serbs havnt run away with you, have they?

LOUKA: No, sir.

PETKOFF: Thats right. Have you brought me some cognac?

LOUKA [*putting the bottle on the table*] Here, sir.

PETKOFF: Thats right. [*He pours some into his coffee*].

Catherine, who, having at this early hour made only a very perfunctory toilet, wears a Bulgarian apron over a once brilliant but now half worn-out dressing gown, and a colored handkerchief tied over her thick black hair, comes from the house with Turkish slippers on her bare feet, looking astonishingly handsome and stately under all the circumstances. Louka goes into the house.

CATHERINE: My dear Paul: what a surprise for us! [*She stoops over the back of his chair to kiss him*]. Have they brought you fresh coffee?

PETKOFF: Yes: Louka's been looking after me. The war's over. The treaty was signed three days ago at Bucharest; and the decree for our army to demobilize was issued yesterday.

CATHERINE [*springing erect, with flashing eyes*] Paul: have you let the Austrians force you to make peace?

PETKOFF [*submissively*] My dear: they didnt consult me. What could I do? [*She sits down and turns away from him*] But of course we saw to it that the treaty was an honorable one. It declares peace—

CATHERINE [*outraged*] Peace!

PETKOFF [*appeasing her*]—but not friendly relations: remember that. They wanted to put that in; but I insisted on its being struck out. What more could I do?

CATHERINE: You could have annexed Serbia and made Prince Alexander Emperor of the Balkans. Thats what I would have done.

PETKOFF: I dont doubt it in the least, my dear. But I should have had to subdue the whole Austrian Empire first; and that would have kept me too long away from you. I missed you greatly.

CATHERINE [*relenting*] Ah! [*She stretches her hand affectionately across the table to squeeze his*].

PETKOFF: And how have you been, my dear?

CATHERINE: Oh, my usual sore throats: thats all.

PETKOFF [*with conviction*] That comes from washing your neck every day. Ive often told you so.

CATHERINE: Nonsense, Paul!

PETKOFF [*over his coffee and cigaret*] I dont believe in going too far with these modern customs. All this washing cant be good for the health: it's not natural. There was an Englishman at Philippopolis who used to wet himself all over with cold water every morning when he got up. Disgusting! It all comes from the English: their climate makes them so dirty that they have to be perpetually washing themselves. Look at my father! he never had a bath in his life; and he lived to be ninety-eight, the healthiest man in Bulgaria. I dont mind a good wash once a week to keep up my position; but once a day is carrying the thing to a ridiculous extreme.

CATHERINE: You are a barbarian at heart still, Paul. I hope you behaved yourself before all those Russian officers.

PETKOFF: I did my best. I took care to let them know that we have a library.

CATHERINE: Ah; but you didnt tell them that we have an electric bell in it? I have had one put up.

PETKOFF: Whats an electric bell?

CATHERINE: You touch a button; something tinkles in the kitchen; and then Nicola comes up.

PETKOFF: Why not shout for him?

CATHERINE: Civilized people never shout for their servants. Ive learnt that while you were away.

PETKOFF: Well, I'll tell you something Ive learnt too. Civilized people dont hang out their washing to dry where visitors can see it; so youd better have all that [*indicating the clothes on the bushes*] put somewhere else.

CATHERINE: Oh, thats absurd, Paul: I dont believe really refined people notice such things.

SERGIUS [*knocking at the stable gates*] Gate, Nicola!

PETKOFF: Theres Sergius. [*Shouting*] Hollo, Nicola!

CATHERINE: Oh, dont shout, Paul: it really isnt nice.

PETKOFF: Bosh! [*He shouts louder than before*] Nicola!

NICOLA [*appearing at the house door*] Yes, sir.

PETKOFF: Are you deaf? Dont you hear Major Saranoff knocking? Bring him round this way. [*He pronounces the name with the stress on the second syllable: Sarahnoff*].

NICOLA: Yes, Major. [*He goes into the stable yard*].

PETKOFF: You must talk to him, my dear, until Raina takes him off our hands. He bores my life out about our not promoting him. Over my head, if you please.

CATHERINE: He certainly ought to be promoted when he marries Raina. Besides, the country should insist on having at least one native general.

PETKOFF: Yes; so that he could throw away whole brigades instead of regiments. It's no use, my dear: he hasnt the slightest chance of promotion until we're quite sure that the peace will be a lasting one.

NICOLA [*at the gate, announcing*] Major Sergius Saranoff! [*He goes into the house and returns presently with a third chair, which he places at the table. He then withdraws*].

Major Sergius Saranoff, the original of the portrait in Raina's room, is a tall romantically handsome man, with the physical hardihood, the high spirit, and the susceptible imagination of an untamed mountaineer chieftain. But his remarkable personal distinction is of a characteristically civilized type. The ridges of his eyebrows, curving with an interrogative twist round the projections at the outer corners; his jealously observant eye; his nose, thin, keen, and apprehensive in spite of the pugnacious high bridge and large nostril; his assertive chin would not be out of place in a Parisian salon, shewing that the clever imaginative barbarian has an acute

*critical faculty which has been thrown into intense activity
by the arrival of western civilization in the Balkans. The result is precisely what the advent of nineteenth century
thought first produced in England: to wit, Byronism. By his
brooding on the perpetual failure, not only of others, but of
himself, to live up to his ideals; by his consequent cynical
scorn for humanity; by his jejune credulity as to the absolute
validity of his concepts and the unworthiness of the world in
disregarding them; by his wincings and mockeries under the
sting of the petty disillusions which every hour spent among
men brings to his sensitive observation, he has acquired the
half tragic, half ironic air, the mysterious moodiness, the suggestion of a strange and terrible history that has left nothing
but undying remorse, by which Childe Harold fascinated the
grandmothers of his English contemporaries. It is clear that
here or nowhere is Raina's ideal hero. Catherine is hardly
less enthusiastic about him than her daughter, and much less
reserved in shewing her enthusiasm. As he enters from the
stable gate, she rises effusively to greet him. Petkoff is dis-
tinctly less disposed to make a fuss about him.*

PETKOFF: Here already, Sergius! Glad to see you.

CATHERINE: My dear Sergius! [*She holds out both her hands*].

SERGIUS [*kissing them with scrupulous gallantry*] My dear
mother, if I may call you so.

PETKOFF [*drily*] Mother-in-law, Sergius: mother-in-law! Sit
down; and have some coffee.

SERGIUS: Thank you: none for me. [*He gets away from the
table with a certain distaste for Petkoff's enjoyment of it, and
posts himself with conscious dignity against the rail of the
steps leading to the house*].

CATHERINE: You look superb. The campaign has improved
you, Sergius. Everybody here is mad about you. We were all
wild with enthusiasm about that magnificent cavalry charge.

SERGIUS [*with grave irony*] Madam: it was the cradle and the
grave of my military reputation.

CATHERINE: How so?

SERGIUS: I won the battle the wrong way when our worthy

Russian generals were losing it the right way. In short, I upset their plans, and wounded their self-esteem. Two Cossack colonels had their regiments routed on the most correct principles of scientific warfare. Two major-generals got killed strictly according to military etiquette. The two colonels are now major-generals; and I am still a simple major.

CATHERINE: You shall not remain so, Sergius. The women are on your side; and they will see that justice is done you.

SERGIUS: It is too late. I have only waited for the peace to send in my resignation.

PETKOFF [*dropping his cup in his amazement*] Your resignation!

CATHERINE: Oh, you must withdraw it!

SERGIUS [*with resolute measured emphasis, folding his arms*] I never withdraw.

PETKOFF [*vexed*] Now who could have supposed you were going to do such a thing?

SERGIUS [*with fire*] Everyone that knew me. But enough of myself and my affairs. How is Raina; and where is Raina?

RAINA [*suddenly coming round the corner of the house and standing at the top of the steps in the path*] Raina is here.

   She makes a charming picture as they turn to look at her. She wears an underdress of pale green silk, draped with an overdress of thin ecru canvas embroidered with gold. She is crowned with a dainty eastern cap of gold tinsel. Sergius goes impulsively to meet her. Posing regally, she presents her hand: he drops chivalrously on one knee and kisses it.

PETKOFF [*aside to Catherine, beaming with parental pride*] Pretty, isn't it? She always appears at the right moment.

CATHERINE [*impatiently*] Yes; she listens for it. It is an abominable habit.

   Sergius leads Raina forward with splendid gallantry. When they arrive at the table, she turns to him with a bend of the head: he bows; and thus they separate, he coming to his place, and she going behind her father's chair.

RAINA [*stooping and kissing her father*] Dear father! Welcome home!

PETKOFF [*patting her cheek*] My little pet girl. [*He kisses her. She goes to the chair left by Nicola for Sergius, and sits down*].

CATHERINE: And so youre no longer a soldier, Sergius.

SERGIUS: I am no longer a soldier. Soldiering, my dear madam, is the coward's art of attacking mercilessly when you are strong, and keeping out of harm's way when you are weak. That is the whole secret of successful fighting. Get your enemy at a disadvantage; and never, on any account, fight him on equal terms.

PETKOFF: They wouldnt let us make a fair stand-up fight of it. However, I suppose soldiering has to be a trade like any other trade.

SERGIUS: Precisely. But I have no ambition to shine as a tradesman; so I have taken the advice of that bagman of a captain that settled the exchange of prisoners with us at Pirot, and given it up.

PETKOFF: What! that Swiss fellow? Sergius: Ive often thought of that exchange since. He over-reached us about those horses.

SERGIUS: Of course he over-reached us. His father was a hotel and livery stable keeper; and he owed his first step to his knowledge of horse-dealing. [*With mock enthusiasm*] Ah, he was a soldier: every inch a soldier! If only I had bought the horses for my regiment instead of foolishly leading it into danger, I should have been a field-marshal now!

CATHERINE: A Swiss? What was he doing in the Serbian army?

PETKOFF: A volunteer, of course: keen on picking up his profession. [*Chuckling*] We shouldnt have been able to begin fighting if these foreigners hadnt shewn us how to do it: we knew nothing about it; and neither did the Serbs. Egad, there'd have been no war without them!

RAINA: Are there many Swiss officers in the Serbian Army?

PETKOFF: No. All Austrians, just as our officers were all Russians. This was the only Swiss I came across. I'll never trust a Swiss again. He humbugged us into giving him fifty ablebodied men for two hundred worn out chargers. They werent even eatable!

SERGIUS: We were two children in the hands of that consummate soldier, Major: simply two innocent little children.

RAINA: What was he like?

CATHERINE: Oh, Raina, what a silly question!

SERGIUS: He was like a commercial traveller in uniform. Bourgeois to his boots!

PETKOFF [*grinning*] Sergius: tell Catherine that queer story his friend told us about how he escaped after Slivnitza. You remember. About his being hid by two women.

SERGIUS [*with bitter irony*] Oh yes: quite a romance! He was serving in the very battery I so unprofessionally charged. Being a thorough soldier, he ran away like the rest of them, with our cavalry at his heels. To escape their sabres he climbed a waterpipe and made his way into the bedroom of a young Bulgarian lady. The young lady was enchanted by his persuasive commercial traveller's manners. She very modestly entertained him for an hour or so, and then called in her mother lest her conduct should appear unmaidenly. The old lady was equally fascinated; and the fugitive was sent on his way in the morning, disguised in an old coat belonging to the master of the house, who was away at the war.

RAINA [*rising with marked stateliness*] Your life in the camp has made you coarse, Sergius. I did not think you would have repeated such a story before me. [*She turns away coldly*].

CATHERINE [*also rising*] She is right, Sergius. If such women exist, we should be spared the knowledge of them.

PETKOFF: Pooh! nonsense! what does it matter?

SERGIUS [*ashamed*] No, Petkoff: I was wrong. [*To Raina, with earnest humility*] I beg your pardon. I have behaved abominably. Forgive me, Raina. [*She bows reservedly*]. And you too, madam. [*Catherine bows graciously and sits down. He proceeds solemnly, again addressing Raina*] The glimpses I have had of the seamy side of life during the last few months have made me cynical; but I should not have brought my cynicism here: least of all into your presence, Raina. I— [*Here, turning to the others, he is evidently going to begin a long speech when the Major interrupts him*].

PETKOFF: Stuff and nonsense, Sergius! Thats quite enough fuss about nothing: a soldier's daughter should be able to stand up without flinching to a little strong conversation. [*He rises*]. Come: it's time for us to get to business. We have to make up our minds how those three regiments are to get back to Philippopolis: theres no forage for them on the Sofia route. [*He goes towards the house*]. Come along. [*Sergius is about to follow him when Catherine rises and intervenes*].

CATHERINE: Oh, Paul, cant you spare Sergius for a few moments? Raina has hardly seen him yet. Perhaps I can help you to settle about the regiments.

SERGIUS [*protesting*] My dear madam, impossible: you—

CATHERINE [*stopping him playfully*] You stay here, my dear Sergius: theres no hurry. I have a word or two to say to Paul. [*Sergius instantly bows and steps back*]. Now, dear [*taking Petkoff's arm*]: come and see the electric bell.

PETKOFF: Oh, very well, very well.

    They go into the house together affectionately. Sergius, left alone with Raina, looks anxiously at her, fearing that she is still offended. She smiles, and stretches out her arms to him.

SERGIUS [*hastening to her*] Am I forgiven?

RAINA [*placing her hands on his shoulders as she looks up at him with admiration and worship*] My hero! My king!

SERGIUS: My queen! [*He kisses her on the forehead*].

RAINA: How I have envied you, Sergius! You have been out in the world, on the field of battle, able to prove yourself there worthy of any woman in the world; whilst I have had to sit at home inactive—dreaming—useless—doing nothing that could give me the right to call myself worthy of any man.

SERGIUS: Dearest: all my deeds have been yours. You inspired me. I have gone through the war like a knight in a tournament with his lady looking down at him!

RAINA: And you have never been absent from my thoughts for a moment. [*Very solemnly*] Sergius: I think we two have found the higher love. When I think of you, I feel that I could never do a base deed, or think an ignoble thought.

SERGIUS: My lady and my saint! [*He clasps her reverently*].

RAINA [*returning his embrace*] My lord and my—

SERGIUS: Sh—sh! Let me be the worshipper, dear. You little know how unworthy even the best man is of a girl's pure passion!

RAINA: I trust you. I love you. You will never disappoint me, Sergius. [*Louka is heard singing within the house. They quickly release each other*]. I cant pretend to talk indifferently before her: my heart is too full. [*Louka comes from the house with her tray. She goes to the table, and begins to clear it, with her back turned to them*]. I will get my hat; and then we can go out until lunch time. Wouldnt you like that?

SERGIUS: Be quick. If you are away five minutes, it will seem five hours. [*Raina runs to the top of the steps, and turns there to exchange looks with him and wave him a kiss with both hands. He looks after her with emotion for a moment; then turns slowly away, his face radiant with the loftiest exaltation. The movement shifts his field of vision, into the corner of which there now comes the tail of Louka's double apron. His attention is arrested at once. He takes a stealthy look at her, and begins to twirl his moustache mischievously, with his left hand akimbo on his hip. Finally, striking the ground with his heels in something of a cavalry swagger, he strolls over to the other side of the table, opposite her, and says*] Louka: do you know what the higher love is?

LOUKA [*astonished*] No, sir.

SERGIUS: Very fatiguing thing to keep up for any length of time, Louka. One feels the need of some relief after it.

LOUKA [*innocently*] Perhaps you would like some coffee, sir? [*She stretches her hand across the table for the coffee pot*].

SERGIUS [*taking her hand*] Thank you, Louka.

LOUKA [*pretending to pull*] Oh, sir, you know I didnt mean that. I'm surprised at you!

SERGIUS [*coming clear of the table and drawing her with him*] I am surprised at myself, Louka. What would Sergius, the hero of Slivnitza, say if he saw me now? What would Sergius, the apostle of the higher love, say if he saw me now? What would the half dozen Sergiuses who keep popping in and out of this handsome figure of mine say if they caught us here? [*Letting go her hand and slipping his arm dexterously round her waist*] Do you consider my figure handsome, Louka?

LOUKA: Let me go, sir. I shall be disgraced. [*She struggles: he holds her inexorably*]. Oh, will you let go?

SERGIUS [*looking straight into her eyes*] No.

LOUKA: Then stand back where we cant be seen. Have you no common sense?

SERGIUS: Ah! thats reasonable. [*He takes her into the stable yard gateway, where they are hidden from the house*].

LOUKA [*plaintively*] I may have been seen from the windows: Miss Raina is sure to be spying about after you.

SERGIUS [*stung: letting her go*] Take care, Louka. I may be worthless enough to betray the higher love; but do not you insult it.

LOUKA [*demurely*] Not for the world, sir, I'm sure. May I go on with my work, please, now?

SERGIUS [*again putting his arm round her*] You are a provoking little witch, Louka. If you were in love with me, would you spy out of windows on me?

LOUKA: Well, you see, sir, since you say you are half a dozen different gentlemen all at once, I should have a great deal to look after.

SERGIUS [*charmed*] Witty as well as pretty. [*He tries to kiss her*].

LOUKA [*avoiding him*] No: I dont want your kisses. Gentlefolk are all alike: you making love to me behind Miss Raina's back; and she doing the same behind yours.

SERGIUS [*recoiling a step*] Louka!

LOUKA: It shews how little you really care.

SERGIUS [*dropping his familiarity, and speaking with freezing politeness*] If our conversation is to continue, Louka, you will please remember that a gentleman does not discuss the conduct of the lady he is engaged to with her maid.

LOUKA: It's so hard to know what a gentleman considers right. I thought from your trying to kiss me that you had given up being so particular.

SERGIUS [*turning from her and striking his forehead as he comes back into the garden from the gateway*] Devil! devil!

LOUKA: Ha! ha! I expect one of the six of you is very like me, sir; though I am only Miss Raina's maid. [*She goes back to her work at the table, taking no further notice of him*].

SERGIUS [*speaking to himself*] Which of the six is the real man? thats the question that torments me. One of them is a hero, another a buffoon, another a humbug, another perhaps a bit of a blackguard. [*He pauses, and looks furtively at Louka as he adds, with deep bitterness*] And one, at least, is a coward: jealous, like all cowards. [*He goes to the table*]. Louka.

LOUKA: Yes?

SERGIUS: Who is my rival?

LOUKA: You shall never get that out of me, for love or money.

SERGIUS: Why?

LOUKA: Never mind why. Besides, you would tell that I told you; and I should lose my place.

SERGIUS [*holding out his right hand in affirmation*] No! on the honor of a—[*He checks himself; and his hand drops, nerveless, as he concludes sardonically*]—of a man capable of behaving as I have been behaving for the last five minutes. Who is he?

LOUKA: I dont know. I never saw him. I only heard his voice through the door of her room.

SERGIUS: Damnation! How dare you?

LOUKA [*retreating*] Oh, I mean no harm: youve no right to take up my words like that. The mistress knows all about it. And I tell you that if that gentleman ever comes here again, Miss Raina will marry him, whether he likes it or not. I know the difference between the sort of manner you and she put on before one another and the real manner.

Sergius shivers as if she had stabbed him. Then, setting his face like iron, he strides grimly to her, and grips her above the elbows with both hands.

SERGIUS: Now listen you to me.

LOUKA [*wincing*] Not so tight: youre hurting me.

SERGIUS: That doesnt matter. You have stained my honor by making me a party to your eavesdropping. And you have betrayed your mistress.

LOUKA [*writhing*] Please—

SERGIUS: That shews that you are an abominable little clod of common clay, with the soul of a servant. [*He lets her go as if she were an unclean thing, and turns away, dusting his hands of her, to the bench by the wall, where he sits down with averted head, meditating gloomily*].

LOUKA [*whimpering angrily with her hands up her sleeves, feeling her bruised arms*] You know how to hurt with your tongue as well as with your hands. But I dont care, now Ive found out that whatever clay I'm made of, youre made of the same. As for her, she's a liar; and her fine airs are a cheat; and I'm worth six of her. [*She shakes the pain off hardily; tosses her head; and sets to work to put the things on the tray*].

He looks doubtfully at her. She finishes packing the tray, and laps the cloth over the edges, so as to carry all out together. As she stoops to lift it, he rises.

SERGIUS: Louka! [*She stops and looks defiantly at him*]. A gentleman has no right to hurt a woman under any circumstances. [*With profound humility, uncovering his head*] I beg your pardon.

LOUKA: That sort of apology may satisfy a lady. Of what use is it to a servant?

SERGIUS [*rudely crossed in his chivalry, throws it off with a bitter laugh, and says slightingly*] Oh! you wish to be paid for the hurt? [*He puts on his shako, and takes some money from his pocket*].

LOUKA [*her eyes filling with tears in spite of herself*] No: I want my hurt made well.

SERGIUS [*sobered by her tone*] How?

She rolls up her left sleeve; clasps her arm with the thumb and fingers of her right hand; and looks down at the bruise. Then she raises her head and looks straight at him. Finally, with a superb gesture, she presents her arm to be kissed.

Amazed, he looks at her; at the arm; at her again; hesitates; and then, with shuddering intensity, exclaims Never! *and gets away as far as possible from her.*

Her arm drops. Without a word, and with unaffected dignity, she takes her tray, and is approaching the house when Raina returns, wearing a hat and jacket in the height of the Vienna fashion of the previous year, 1885. Louka makes way proudly for her, and then goes into the house.

RAINA: I'm ready. Whats the matter? [*Gaily*] Have you been flirting with Louka?

SERGIUS [*hastily*] No, no. How can you think such a thing?

RAINA [*ashamed of herself*] Forgive me, dear: it was only a jest. I am so happy today.

He goes quickly to her, and kisses her hand remorsefully. Catherine comes out and calls to them from the top of the steps.

CATHERINE [*coming down to them*] I am sorry to disturb you, children; but Paul is distracted over those three regiments. He doesnt know how to send them to Philippopolis; and he objects to every suggestion of mine. You must go and help him, Sergius. He is in the library.

RAINA [*disappointed*] But we are just going out for a walk.

SERGIUS: I shall not be long. Wait for me just five minutes. [*He runs up the steps to the door*].

RAINA [*following him to the foot of the steps and looking up at him with timid coquetry*] I shall go round and wait in full view of the library windows. Be sure you draw father's attention to me. If you are a moment longer than five minutes, I shall go in and fetch you, regiments or no regiments.

SERGIUS [*laughing*] Very well. [*He goes in*].

Raina watches him until he is out of her sight. Then, with a perceptible relaxation of manner, she begins to pace up and down the garden in a brown study.

CATHERINE: Imagine their meeting that Swiss and hearing the whole story! The very first thing your father asked for was the old coat we sent him off in. A nice mess you have got us into!

RAINA [*gazing thoughtfully at the gravel as she walks*] The little beast!

CATHERINE: Little beast! What little beast?

RAINA: To go and tell! Oh, if I had him here, I'd cram him with chocolate creams til he couldnt ever speak again!

CATHERINE: Dont talk such stuff. Tell me the truth, Raina. How long was he in your room before you came to me?

RAINA [*whisking round and recommencing her march in the opposite direction*] Oh, I forget.

CATHERINE: You cannot forget! Did he really climb up after the soldiers were gone; or was he there when that officer searched the room?

RAINA: No. Yes: I think he must have been there then.

CATHERINE: You think! Oh, Raina! Raina! Will anything ever make you straightforward? If Sergius finds out, it will be all over between you.

RAINA [*with cool imipertinence*] Oh, I know Sergius is your pet. I sometimes wish you could marry him instead of me. You would just suit him. You would pet him, and spoil him, and mother him to perfection.

CATHERINE [*opening her eyes very widely indeed*] Well, upon my word!

RAINA [*capriciously: half to herself*] I always feel a longing to do or say something dreadful to him—to shock his propriety—to scandalize the five senses out of him. [*To Catherine, perversely*] I dont care whether he finds out about the chocolate cream soldier or not. I half hope he may. [*She again turns and strolls flippantly away up the path to the corner of the house*].

CATHERINE: And what should I be able to say to your father, pray?

RAINA [*over her shoulder, from the top of the two steps*] Oh, poor father! As if he could help himself! [*She turns the corner and passes out of sight*].

CATHERINE [*looking after her, her fingers itching*] Oh, if you were only ten years younger! [*Louka comes from the house*

with a salver, which she carries hanging down by her side].
Well?

LOUKA: Theres a gentleman just called, madam. A Serbian officer.

CATHERINE [*flaming*] A Serb! And how dare he—[*checking herself bitterly*] Oh, I forgot. We are at peace now. I suppose we shall have them calling every day to pay their compliments. Well: if he is an officer why dont you tell your master? He is in the library with Major Saranoff. Why do you come to me?

LOUKA: But he asks for you, madam. And I dont think he knows who you are: he said the lady of the house. He gave me this little ticket for you. [*She takes a card out of her bosom; puts it on the salver; and offers it to Catherine*].

CATHERINE [*reading*] "Captain Bluntschli"? Thats a German name.

LOUKA: Swiss, madam, I think.

CATHERINE [*with a bound that makes Louka jump back*] Swiss! What is he like?

LOUKA [*timidly*] He has a big carpet bag, madam.

CATHERINE: Oh Heavens! he's come to return the coat. Send him away: say we're not at home: ask him to leave his address and I'll write to him. Oh stop: that will never do. Wait! [*She throws herself into a chair to think it out. Louka waits*]. The master and Major Saranoff are busy in the library, arnt they?

LOUKA: Yes, madam.

CATHERINE [*decisively*] Bring the gentleman out here at once. [*Peremptorily*] And be very polite to him. Dont delay. Here [*impatiently snatching the salver from her*]: leave that here; and go straight back to him.

LOUKA: Yes, madam [*going*].

CATHERINE: Louka!

LOUKA [*stopping*] Yes, madam.

CATHERINE: Is the library door shut?

LOUKA: I think so, madam.

CATHERINE: If not, shut it as you pass through.

LOUKA: Yes, madam [*going*].

CATHERINE: Stop [*Louka stops*]. He will have to go that way [*indicating the gate of the stable yard*]. Tell Nicola to bring his bag here after him. Dont forget.

LOUKA [*surprised*] His bag?

CATHERINE: Yes: here: as soon as possible. [*Vehemently*] Be quick! [*Louka runs into the house. Catherine snatches her apron off and throws it behind a bush. She then takes up the salver and uses it as a mirror, with the result that the handkerchief tied round her head follows the apron. A touch to her hair and a shake to her dressing gown make her presentable*]. Oh, how? how? how can a man be such a fool! Such a moment to select! [*Louka appears at the door of the house, announcing* Captain Bluntschli. *She stands aside at the top of the steps to let him pass before she goes in again. He is the man of the midnight adventure in Raina's room, clean, well brushed, smartly uniformed, and out of trouble, but still unmistakably the same man. The moment Louka's back is turned, Catherine swoops on him with impetuous, urgent, coaxing appeal*]. Captain Bluntschli: I am very glad to see you; but you must leave this house at once. [*He raises his eyebrows*]. My husband has just returned with my future son-in-law; and they know nothing. If they did, the consequences would be terrible. You are a foreigner: you do not feel our national animosities as we do. We still hate the Serbs: the effect of the peace on my husband has been to make him feel like a lion baulked of his prey. If he discovers our secret, he will never forgive me; and my daughter's life will hardly be safe. Will you, like the chivalrous gentleman and soldier you are, leave at once before he finds you here?

BLUNTSCHLI [*disappointed, but philosophical*] At once, gracious lady. I only came to thank you and return the coat you lent me. If you will allow me to take it out of my bag and leave it with your servant as I pass out, I need detain you no further. [*He turns to go into the house*].

CATHERINE [*catching him by the sleeve*] Oh, you must not think of going back that way. [*Coaxing him across to the sta-*

ble gates] This is the shortest way out. Many thanks. So glad to have been of service to you. Good-bye.

BLUNTSCHLI: But my bag?

CATHERINE: It shall be sent on. You will leave me your address.

BLUNTSCHLI: True. Allow me. [*He takes out his card-case, and stops to write his address, keeping Catherine in an agony of impatience. As he hands her the card, Petkoff, hatless, rushes from the house in a fluster of hospitality, followed by Sergius*].

PETKOFF [*as he hurries down the steps*] My dear Captain Bluntschli—

CATHERINE: Oh Heavens! [*She sinks on the seat against the wall*].

PETKOFF [*too preoccupied to notice her as he shakes Bluntschli's hand heartily*] Those stupid people of mine thought I was out here, instead of in the—haw!—library [*he cannot mention the library without betraying how proud he is of it*]. I saw you through the window. I was wondering why you didnt come in. Saranoff is with me: you remember him, dont you?

SERGIUS [*saluting humorously, and then offering his hand with great charm of manner*] Welcome, our friend the enemy!

PETKOFF: No longer the enemy, happily. [*Rather anxiously*] I hope youve called as a friend, and not about horses or prisoners.

CATHERINE: Oh, quite as a friend, Paul. I was just asking Captain Bluntschli to stay to lunch; but he declares he must go at once.

SERGIUS [*sardonically*] Impossible, Bluntschli. We want you here badly. We have to send on three cavalry regiments to Philippopolis; and we dont in the least know how to do it.

BLUNTSCHLI [*suddenly attentive and businesslike*] Philippopolis? The forage is the trouble, I suppose.

PETKOFF [*eagerly*] Yes: thats it. [*To Sergius*] He sees the whole thing at once.

BLUNTSCHLI: I think I can shew you how to manage that.

SERGIUS: Invaluable man! Come along! [*Towering over Bluntschli, he puts his hand on his shoulder and takes him to the steps, Petkoff following*].

    Raina comes from the house as Bluntschli puts his foot on the first step.

RAINA: Oh! The chocolate cream soldier!

    Bluntschli stands rigid. Sergius, amazed, looks at Raina, then at Petkoff, who looks back at him and then at his wife.

CATHERINE [*with commanding presence of mind*] My dear Raina, dont you see that we have a guest here? Captain Bluntschli: one of our new Serbian friends.

    Raina bows: Bluntschli bows.

RAINA: How silly of me! [*She comes down into the centre of the group, between Bluntschli and Petkoff*]. I made a beautiful ornament this morning for the ice pudding; and that stupid Nicola has just put down a pile of plates on it and spoilt it. [*To Bluntschli, winningly*] I hope you didnt think that you were the chocolate cream soldier, Captain Bluntschli.

BLUNTSCHLI [*laughing*] I assure you I did. [*Stealing a whimsical glance at her*] Your explanation was a relief.

PETKOFF [*suspiciously, to Raina*] And since when, pray, have you taken to cooking?

CATHERINE: Oh, whilst you were away. It is her latest fancy.

PETKOFF [*testily*] And has Nicola taken to drinking? He used to be careful enough. First he shews Captain Bluntschli out here when he knew quite well I was in the library; and then he goes downstairs and breaks Raina's chocolate soldier. He must—[*Nicola appears at the top of the steps with the bag. He descends; places it respectfully before Bluntschli; and waits for further orders. General amazement. Nicola, unconscious of the effect he is producing, looks perfectly satisfied with himself. When Petkoff recovers his power of speech, he breaks out at him with*] Are you mad, Nicola?

NICOLA [*taken aback*] Sir?

PETKOFF: What have you brought that for?

NICOLA: My lady's orders, major. Louka told me that—

CATHERINE [*interrupting him*] My orders! Why should I order you to bring Captain Bluntschli's luggage out here? What are you thinking of, Nicola?

NICOLA [*after a moment's bewilderment, picking up the bag as he addresses Bluntschli with the very perfection of servile discretion*] I beg your pardon, captain, I am sure. [*To Catherine*] My fault, madam: I hope youll overlook it. [*He bows, and is going to the steps with the bag, when Petkoff addresses him angrily*].

PETKOFF: Youd better go and slam that bag, too, down on Miss Raina's ice pudding! [*This is too much for Nicola. The bag drops from his hand almost on his master's toes, eliciting a roar of*] Begone, you butter-fingered donkey.

NICOLA [*snatching up the bag, and escaping into the house*] Yes, major.

CATHERINE: Oh, never mind. Paul: dont be angry.

PETKOFF [*blustering*] Scoundrel! He's got out of hand while I was away. I'll teach him. Infernal blackguard! The sack next Saturday! I'll clear out the whole establishment—[*He is stifled by the caresses of his wife and daughter, who hang round his neck, petting him*].

CATHERINE } [*together*] { Now, now, now, it mustnt be
RAINA   }   { Wow, wow, wow: not on your

{ angry. He meant no harm. Be good to
{ first day at home. I'll make another ice
{ please me, dear. Sh-sh-sh-sh!
{ pudding. Tch-ch-ch!

PETKOFF [*yielding*] Oh well, never mind. Come, Bluntschli: lets have no more nonsense about going away. You know very well youre not going back to Switzerland yet. Until you do go back youll stay with us.

RAINA: Oh, do, Captain Bluntschli.

PETKOFF [*to Catherine*] Now, Catherine: it's of you he's afraid. Press him; and he'll stay.

CATHERINE: Of course I shall be only too delighted if [*appealingly*] Captain Bluntschli really wishes to stay. He knows my wishes.

BLUNTSCHLI [*in his driest military manner*] I am at madam's
  orders.
SERGIUS [*cordially*] That settles it!
PETKOFF [*heartily*] Of course!
RAINA: You see you must stay.
BLUNTSCHLI [*smiling*] Well, if I must, I must.
  Gesture of despair from Catherine.

ACT III

In the library after lunch. It is not much of a library. Its literary equipment consists of a single fixed shelf stocked with old paper covered novels, broken backed, coffee stained, torn and thumbed; and a couple of little hanging shelves with a few gift books on them: the rest of the wall space being occupied by trophies of war and the chase. But it is a most comfortable sitting room. A row of three large windows shews a mountain panorama, just now seen in one of its friendliest aspects in the mellowing afternoon light. In the corner next the right hand window a square earthenware stove, a perfect tower of glistening pottery, rises nearly to the ceiling and guarantees plenty of warmth. The ottoman is like that in Raina's room, and similarly placed; and the window seats are luxurious with decorated cushions. There is one object, however, hopelessly out of keeping with its surroundings. This is a small kitchen table, much the worse for wear, fitted as a writing table with an old canister full of pens, an eggcup filled with ink, and a deplorable scrap of heavily used pink blotting paper.

At the side of this table, which stands to the left of anyone facing the window, Bluntschli is hard at work with a couple of maps before him, writing orders. At the head of it sits Sergius, who is supposed to be also at work, but is actually gnawing the feather of a pen, and contemplating Bluntschli's quick, sure, businesslike progress with a mixture of envious irritation at his own incapacity and awestruck wonder at an

*ability which seems to him almost miraculous, though its
prosaic character forbids him to esteem it. The Major is comfortably established on the ottoman, with a newspaper in his
hand and the tube of his hookah within easy reach. Catherine sits at the stove, with her back to them, embroidering.
Raina, reclining on the divan, is gazing in a daydream out at
the Balkan landscape, with a neglected novel in her lap.*

*The door is on the same side as the stove, farther from the
window. The button of the electric bell is at the opposite
side, behind Bluntschli.*

PETKOFF [*looking up from his paper to watch how they are
getting on at the table*] Are you sure I cant help you in any
way, Bluntschli?

BLUNTSCHLI [*without interrupting his writing or looking up*]
Quite sure, thank you. Saranoff and I will manage it.

SERGIUS [*grimly*] Yes: we'll manage it. He finds out what to do;
draws up the orders; and I sign em. Division of labor!
[*Bluntschli passes him a paper*]. Another one? Thank you.
[*He plants the paper squarely before him; sets his chair care-
fully parallel to it; and signs with his cheek on his elbow and
his protruded tongue following the movements of his pen*].
This hand is more accustomed to the sword than to the pen.

PETKOFF: It's very good of you, Bluntschli: it is indeed, to let
yourself be put upon in this way. Now are you quite sure I
can do nothing?

CATHERINE [*in a low warning tone*] You can stop interrupting,
Paul.

PETKOFF [*starting and looking round at her*] Eh? Oh! Quite
right, my love: quite right. [*He takes his newspaper up again,
but presently lets it drop*]. Ah, you havnt been campaigning,
Catherine: you dont know how pleasant it is for us to sit
here, after a good lunch, with nothing to do but enjoy ourselves. Theres only one thing I want to make me thoroughly
comfortable.

CATHERINE: What is that?

PETKOFF: My old coat. I'm not at home in this one: I feel as if I were on parade.

CATHERINE: My dear Paul, how absurd you are about that old coat! It must be hanging in the blue closet where you left it.

PETKOFF: My dear Catherine, I tell you Ive looked there. Am I to believe my own eyes or not? [*Catherine rises and crosses the room to press the button of the electric bell*]. What are you shewing off that bell for? [*She looks at him majestically, and silently resumes her chair and her needlework*]. My dear: if you think the obstinacy of your sex can make a coat out of two old dressing gowns of Raina's, your waterproof, and my mackintosh, youre mistaken. Thats exactly what the blue closet contains at present.

    Nicola presents himself.

CATHERINE: Nicola: go to the blue closet and bring your master's old coat here: the braided one he wears in the house.

NICOLA: Yes, madam. [*He goes out*].

PETKOFF: Catherine.

CATHERINE: Yes, Paul.

PETKOFF: I bet you any piece of jewellery you like to order from Sofia against a week's housekeeping money that the coat isnt there.

CATHERINE: Done, Paul!

PETKOFF [*excited by the prospect of a gamble*] Come: heres an opportunity for some sport. Wholl bet on it? Bluntschli: I'll give you six to one.

BLUNTSCHLI [*imperturbably*] It would be robbing you, major. Madam is sure to be right. [*Without looking up, he passes another batch of papers to Sergius*].

SERGIUS [*also excited*] Bravo, Switzerland! Major: I bet my best charger against an Arab mare for Raina that Nicola finds the coat in the blue closet.

PETKOFF [*eagerly*] Your best char—

CATHERINE [*hastily interrupting him*] Dont be foolish, Paul. An Arabian mare will cost you 50,000 levas.

RAINA [*suddenly coming out of her picturesque revery*] Really, mother, if you are going to take the jewellery, I dont see why you should grudge me my Arab.

Nicola comes back with the coat, and brings it to Petkoff, who can hardly believe his eyes.

CATHERINE: Where was it, Nicola?

NICOLA: Hanging in the blue closet, madam.

PETKOFF: Well, I am d—

CATHERINE [*stopping him*] Paul!

PETKOFF: I could have sworn it wasnt there. Age is beginning to tell on me. I'm getting hallucinations. [*To Nicola*] Here: help me to change. Excuse me, Bluntschli. [*He begins changing coats, Nicola acting as valet*]. Remember: I didnt take that bet of yours, Sergius. Youd better give Raina that Arab steed yourself, since youve roused her expectations. Eh, Raina? [*He looks round at her; but she is again rapt in the landscape. With a little gush of parental affection and pride, he points her out to them, and says*] She's dreaming, as usual.

SERGIUS: Assuredly she shall not be the loser.

PETKOFF: So much the better for her. *I* shant come off so cheaply, I expect. [*The change is now complete. Nicola goes out with the discarded coat*]. Ah, now I feel at home at last. [*He sits down and takes his newspaper with a grunt of relief*].

BLUNTSCHLI [*to Sergius, handing a paper*] Thats the last order.

PETKOFF [*jumping up*] What! Finished?

BLUNTSCHLI: Finished.

PETKOFF [*with childlike envy*] Havnt you anything for me to sign?

BLUNTSCHLI: Not necessary. His signature will do.

PETKOFF [*inflating his chest and thumping it*] Ah well, I think weve done a thundering good day's work. Can I do anything more?

BLUNTSCHLI: You had better both see the fellows that are to take these. [*Sergius rises*] Pack them off at once; and shew them that Ive marked on the orders the time they should hand them in by. Tell them that if they stop to drink or tell stories—if theyre five minutes late, theyll have the skin taken off their backs.

SERGIUS [*stiffening indignantly*] I'll say so. [*He strides to the door*]. And if one of them is man enough to spit in my face for insulting him, I'll buy his discharge and give him a pension. [*He goes out*].

BLUNTSCHLI [*confidentially*] Just see that he talks to them properly, major, will you?

PETKOFF [*officiously*] Quite right, Bluntschli, quite right. I'll see to it. [*He goes to the door importantly, but hesitates on the threshold*]. By the bye, Catherine, you may as well come too. Theyll be far more frightened of you than of me.

CATHERINE [*putting down her embroidery*] I daresay I had better. You would only splutter at them. [*She goes out, Petkoff holding the door for her and following her*].

BLUNTSCHLI: What an army! They make cannons out of cherry trees; and the officers send for their wives to keep discipline! [*He begins to fold and docket the papers*].

 Raina, who has risen from the divan, marches slowly down the room with her hands clasped behind her, and looks mischievously at him.

RAINA: You look ever so much nicer than when we last met. [*He looks up, surprised*]. What have you done to yourself?

BLUNTSCHLI: Washed; brushed; good night's sleep and breakfast. Thats all.

RAINA: Did you get back safely that morning?

BLUNTSCHLI: Quite, thanks.

RAINA: Were they angry with you for running away from Sergius's charge?

BLUNTSCHLI [*grinning*] No: they were glad; because theyd all just run away themselves.

RAINA [*going to the table, and leaning over it towards him*] It must have made a lovely story for them: all that about me and my room.

BLUNTSCHLI: Capital story. But I only told it to one of them: a particular friend.

RAINA: On whose discretion you could absolutely rely?

BLUNTSCHLI: Absolutely.

RAINA: Hm! He told it all to my father and Sergius the day you exchanged the prisoners. [*She turns away and strolls carelessly across to the other side of the room*].

BLUNTSCHLI [*deeply concerned, and half incredulous*] No! You dont mean that, do you?

RAINA [*turning, with sudden earnestness*] I do indeed. But they dont know that it was in this house you took refuge. If Sergius knew, he would challenge you and kill you in a duel.

BLUNTSCHLI: Bless me! then dont tell him.

RAINA: Please be serious, Captain Bluntschli. Can you not realize what it is to me to deceive him? I want to be quite perfect with Sergius: no meanness, no smallness, no deceit. My relation to him is the one really beautiful and noble part of my life. I hope you can understand that.

BLUNTSCHLI [*sceptically*] You mean that you wouldnt like him to find out that the story about the ice pudding was a— a—a—You know.

RAINA [*wincing*] Ah, dont talk of it in that flippant way. I lied: I know it. But I did it to save your life. He would have killed you. That was the second time I ever uttered a falsehood. [*Bluntschli rises quickly and looks doubtfully and somewhat severely at her*]. Do you remember the first time?

BLUNTSCHLI: I! No. Was I present?

RAINA: Yes; and I told the officer who was searching for you that you were not present.

BLUNTSCHLI: True. I should have remembered it.

RAINA [*greatly encouraged*] Ah, it is natural that you should forget it first. It cost you nothing: it cost me a lie! A lie!

She sits down on the ottoman, looking straight before her with her hands clasped around her knee. Bluntschli, quite touched, goes to the ottoman with a particularly reassuring and considerate air, and sits down beside her.

BLUNTSCHLI: My dear young lady, dont let this worry you. Remember: I'm a soldier. Now what are the two things that happen to a soldier so often that he comes to think nothing of them? One is hearing people tell lies [*Raina recoils*]: the other is getting his life saved in all sorts of ways by all sorts of people.

RAINA [*rising in indignant protest*] And so he becomes a creature incapable of faith and of gratitude.

BLUNTSCHLI [*making a wry face*] Do you like gratitude? I dont. If pity is akin to love, gratitude is akin to the other thing.

RAINA: Gratitude! [*Turning on him*] If you are incapable of gratitude you are incapable of any noble sentiment. Even animals are grateful. Oh, I see now exactly what you think of me! You were not surprised to hear me lie. To you it was something I probably did every day! every hour!! That is how men think of women. [*She paces the room tragically*].

BLUNTSCHLI [*dubiously*] Theres reason in everything. You said youd told only two lies in your whole life. Dear young lady: isnt that rather a short allowance? I'm quite a straight-forward man myself; but it wouldnt last me a whole morning.

RAINA [*staring haughtily at him*] Do you know, sir, that you are insulting me?

BLUNTSCHLI: I cant help it. When you strike that noble attitude and speak in that thrilling voice, I admire you; but I find it impossible to believe a single word you say.

RAINA [*superbly*] Captain Bluntschli!

BLUNTSCHLI [*unmoved*] Yes?

RAINA [*standing over him, as if she could not believe her senses*] Do you mean what you said just now? Do you know what you said just now?

BLUNTSCHLI: I do.

RAINA [*gasping*] I! I!!! [*She points to herself incredulously, meaning "I, Raina Petkoff tell lies!" He meets her gaze unflinchingly. She suddenly sits down beside him, and adds, with a complete change of manner from the heroic to a babyish familiarity*] How did you find me out?

BLUNTSCHLI [*promptly*] Instinct, dear young lady. Instinct, and experience of the world.

RAINA [*wonderingly*] Do you know, you are the first man I ever met who did not take me seriously?

BLUNTSCHLI: You mean, dont you, that I am the first man that has ever taken you quite seriously?

RAINA: Yes: I suppose I do mean that. [*Cosily, quite at her ease with him*] How strange it is to be talked to in such a way! You know, Ive always gone on like that.

BLUNTSCHLI: You mean the—?

RAINA: I mean the noble attitude and the thrilling voice. [*They laugh together*]. I did it when I was a tiny child to my nurse. She believed in it. I do it before my parents. They believe in it. I do it before Sergius. He believes in it.

BLUNTSCHLI: Yes: he's a little in that line himself, isnt he?

RAINA [*startled*] Oh! Do you think so?

BLUNTSCHLI: You know him better than I do.

RAINA: I wonder—I wonder is he? If I thought that—! [*Discouraged*] Ah, well: what does it matter? I suppose, now youve found me out, you despise me.

BLUNTSCHLI [*warmly, rising*] No, my dear young lady, no, no, no a thousand times. It's part of your youth: part of your charm. I'm like all the rest of them: the nurse, your parents, Sergius: I'm your infatuated admirer.

RAINA [*pleased*] Really?

BLUNTSCHLI [*slapping his breast smartly with his hand, German fashion*] Hand aufs Herz! Really and truly.

RAINA [*very happy*] But what did you think of me for giving you my portrait?

BLUNTSCHLI [*astonished*] Your portrait! You never gave me your portrait.

RAINA [*quickly*] Do you mean to say you never got it?

BLUNTSCHLI: No. [*He sits down beside her, with renewed interest, and says, with some complacency*] When did you send it to me?

RAINA [*indignantly*] I did not send it to you. [*She turns her head away, and adds, reluctantly*] It was in the pocket of that coat.

BLUNTSCHLI [*pursing his lips and rounding his eyes*] Oh-o-oh! I never found it. It must be there still.

RAINA [*springing up*] There still! for my father to find the first time he puts his hand in his pocket! Oh, how could you be so stupid?

BLUNTSCHLI [*rising also*] It doesnt matter: I suppose it's only a photograph: how can he tell who it was intended for? Tell him he put it there himself.

RAINA [*bitterly*] Yes: that is so clever! isnt it? [*Distractedly*] Oh! what shall I do?

BLUNTSCHLI: Ah, I see. You wrote something on it. That was rash.

RAINA [*vexed almost to tears*] Oh, to have done such a thing for you, who care no more—except to laugh at me—oh! Are you sure nobody has touched it?

BLUNTSCHLI: Well, I cant be quite sure. You see, I couldnt carry it about with me all the time: one cant take much luggage on active service.

RAINA: What did you do with it?

BLUNTSCHLI: When I got through to Pirot I had to put it in safe keeping somehow. I thought of the railway cloak room; but thats the surest place to get looted in modern warfare. So I pawned it.

RAINA: Pawned it!!!

BLUNTSCHLI: I know it doesnt sound nice; but it was much the safest plan. I redeemed it the day before yesterday. Heaven only knows whether the pawnbroker cleared out the pockets or not.

RAINA [*furious: throwing the words right into his face*] You have a low shopkeeping mind. You think of things that would never come into a gentleman's head.

BLUNTSCHLI [*phlegmatically*] Thats the Swiss national character, dear lady. [*He returns to the table*].

RAINA: Oh, I wish I had never met you. [*She flounces away, and sits at the window fuming*].

  Louka comes in with a heap of letters and telegrams on her salver, and crosses, with her bold free gait, to the table. Her left sleeve is looped up to the shoulder with a brooch, shewing her naked arm, with a broad gilt bracelet covering the bruise.

LOUKA [*to Bluntschli*] For you. [*She empties the salver with a fling on to the table*]. The messenger is waiting. [*She is deter-*

mined not to be civil to an enemy, even if she must bring him his letters].

BLUNTSCHLI [*to Raina*] Will you excuse me: the last postal delivery that reached me was three weeks ago. These are the subsequent accumulations. Four telegrams: a week old. [*He opens one*]. Oho! Bad news!

RAINA [*rising and advancing a little remorsefully*] Bad news?

BLUNTSCHLI: My father's dead. [*He looks at the telegram with his lips pursed, musing on the unexpected change in his arrangements. Louka crosses herself hastily*].

RAINA: Oh, how very sad!

BLUNTSCHLI: Yes: I shall have to start for home in an hour. He has left a lot of big hotels behind him to be looked after. [*He takes up a fat letter in a long blue envelope*]. Here's a whacking letter from the family solicitor. [*He pulls out the enclosures and glances over them*]. Great Heavens! Seventy! Two hundred! [*In a crescendo of dismay*] Four hundred! Four thousand!! Nine thousand six hundred!!! What on earth am I to do with them all?

RAINA [*timidly*] Nine thousand hotels?

BLUNTSCHLI: Hotels! nonsense. If you only knew! Oh, it's too ridiculous! Excuse me: I must give my fellow orders about starting. [*He leaves the room hastily, with the documents in his hand*].

LOUKA [*knowing instinctively that she can annoy Raina by disparaging Bluntschli*] He has not much heart, that Swiss. He has not a word of grief for his poor father.

RAINA [*bitterly*] Grief! A man who has been doing nothing but killing people for years! What does he care? What does any soldier care? [*She goes to the door, restraining her tears with difficulty*].

LOUKA: Major Saranoff has been fighting too; and he has plenty of heart left. [*Raina, at the door, draws herself up haughtily and goes out*]. Aha! I thought you wouldnt get much feeling out of your soldier. [*She is following Raina when Nicola enters with an armful of logs for the stove*].

NICOLA [*grinning amorously at her*] Ive been trying all the af-

ternoon to get a minute alone with you, my girl. [*His countenance changes as he notices her arm*]. Why, what fashion is
that of wearing your sleeve, child?

LOUKA [*proudly*] My own fashion.

NICOLA: Indeed! If the mistress catches you, she'll talk to you.
[*He puts the logs down, and seats himself comfortably on
the ottoman*].

LOUKA: Is that any reason why you should take it on yourself
to talk to me?

NICOLA: Come! dont be so contrairy with me. Ive some good
news for you. [*She sits down beside him. He takes out some
paper money. Louka, with an eager gleam in her eyes, tries
to snatch it; but he shifts it quickly to his left hand, out of her
reach*]. See! a twenty leva bill! Sergius gave me that, out of
pure swagger. A fool and his money are soon parted. Theres
ten levas more. The Swiss gave me that for backing up the
mistress's and Raina's lies about him. He's no fool, he isnt.
You should have heard old Catherine downstairs as polite as
you please to me, telling me not to mind the Major being a
little impatient; for they knew what a good servant I was—
after making a fool and a liar of me before them all! The
twenty will go to our savings; and you shall have the ten to
spend if youll only talk to me so as to remind me I'm a hu-
man being. I get tired of being a servant occasionally.

LOUKA: Yes: sell your manhood for 30 levas, and buy me for
10! [*Rising scornfully*] Keep your money. You were born to
be a servant. I was not. When you set up your shop you will
only be everybody's servant instead of somebody's servant.
[*She goes moodily to the table and seats herself regally in
Sergius's chair*].

NICOLA [*picking up his logs, and going to the stove*] Ah, wait
til you see. We shall have our evenings to ourselves; and I
shall be master in my own house, I promise you. [*He throws
the logs down and kneels at the stove*].

LOUKA: You shall never be master in mine.

NICOLA [*turning, still on his knees, and squatting down rather
forlornly on his calves, daunted by her implacable disdain*]

You have a great ambition in you, Louka. Remember: if any luck comes to you, it was I that made a woman of you.

LOUKA: You!

NICOLA [*scrambling up and going at her*] Yes, me. Who was it made you give up wearing a couple of pounds of false black hair on your head and reddening your lips and cheeks like any other Bulgarian girl! I did. Who taught you to trim your nails, and keep your hands clean, and be dainty about yourself, like a fine Russian lady? Me: do you hear that? me! [*She tosses her head defiantly; and he turns away, adding, more coolly*] Ive often thought that if Raina were out of the way, and you just a little less of a fool and Sergius just a little more of one, you might come to be one of my grandest customers, instead of only being my wife and costing me money.

LOUKA: I believe you would rather be my servant than my husband. You would make more out of me. Oh, I know that soul of yours.

NICOLA [*going closer to her for greater emphasis*] Never you mind my soul; but just listen to my advice. If you want to be a lady, your present behavior to me wont do at all, unless when we're alone. It's too sharp and impudent; and impudence is a sort of familiarity: it shews affection for me. And dont you try being high and mighty with me, either. Youre like all country girls: you think it's genteel to treat a servant the way I treat a stableboy. Thats only your ignorance; and dont you forget it. And dont be so ready to defy everybody. Act as if you expected to have your own way, not as if you expected to be ordered about. The way to get on as a lady is the same as the way to get on as a servant: youve got to know your place: thats the secret of it. And you may depend on me to know my place if you get promoted. Think over it, my girl. I'll stand by you: one servant should always stand by another.

LOUKA [*rising impatiently*] Oh, I must behave in my own way. You take all the courage out of me with your cold-blooded wisdom. Go and put those logs on the fire: thats the sort of thing you understand.

Before Nicola can retort, Sergius comes in. He checks himself a moment on seeing Louka; then goes to the stove.

SERGIUS [*to Nicola*] I am not in the way of your work, I hope.

NICOLA [*in a smooth, elderly manner*] Oh no, sir: thank you kindly. I was only speaking to this foolish girl about her habit of running up here to the library whenever she gets a chance, to look at the books. Thats the worst of her education, sir: it gives her habits above her station. [*To Louka*] Make that table tidy, Louka, for the Major. [*He goes out sedately*].

Louka, without looking at Sergius, pretends to arrange the papers on the table. He crosses slowly to her, and studies the arrangement of her sleeve reflectively.

SERGIUS: Let me see: is there a mark there? [*He turns up the bracelet and sees the bruise made by his grasp. She stands motionless, not looking at him: fascinated, but on her guard*] Ffff! Does it hurt?

LOUKA: Yes.

SERGIUS: Shall I cure it?

LOUKA [*instantly withdrawing herself proudly, but still not looking at him*] No. You cannot cure it now.

SERGIUS [*masterfully*] Quite sure? [*He makes a movement as if to take her in his arms*].

LOUKA: Dont trifle with me, please. An officer should not trifle with a servant.

SERGIUS [*indicating the bruise with a merciless stroke of his forefinger*] That was no trifle, Louka.

LOUKA [*flinching; then looking at him for the first time*] Are you sorry?

SERGIUS [*with measured emphasis, folding his arms*] I am never sorry.

LOUKA [*wistfully*] I wish I could believe a man could be as unlike a woman as that. I wonder are you really a brave man?

SERGIUS [*unaffectedly, relaxing his attitude*] Yes: I am a brave man. My heart jumped like a woman's at the first shot; but in the charge I found that I was brave. Yes: that at least is real about me.

LOUKA: Did you find in the charge that the men whose fathers are poor like mine were any less brave than the men who are rich like you?

SERGIUS [*with bitter levity*] Not a bit. They all slashed and cursed and yelled like heroes. Psha! the courage to rage and kill is cheap. I have an English bull terrier who has as much of that sort of courage as the whole Bulgarian nation, and the whole Russian nation at its back. But he lets my groom thrash him, all the same. Thats your soldier all over! No, Louka: your poor men can cut throats; but they are afraid of their officers; they put up with insults and blows; they stand by and see one another punished like children: aye, and help to do it when they are ordered. And the officers!!! Well [*with a short harsh laugh*] I am an officer. Oh, [*fervently*] give me the man who will defy to the death any power on earth or in heaven that sets itself up against his own will and conscience: he alone is the brave man.

LOUKA: How easy it is to talk! Men never seem to me to grow up: they all have schoolboy's ideas. You dont know what true courage is.

SERGIUS [*ironically*] Indeed! I am willing to be instructed. [*He sits on the ottoman, sprawling magnificently*].

LOUKA: Look at me! How much am I allowed to have my own will? I have to get your room ready for you: to sweep and dust, to fetch and carry. How could that degrade me if it did not degrade you to have it done for you? But [*with subdued passion*] if I were Empress of Russia, above everyone in the world, then!! Ah then, though according to you I could shew no courage at all, you should see, you should see.

SERGIUS: What would you do, most noble Empress?

LOUKA: I would marry the man I loved, which no other queen in Europe has the courage to do. If I loved you, though you would be as far beneath me as I am beneath you, I would dare to be the equal of my inferior. Would you dare as much if you loved me? No: if you felt the beginnings of love for me you would not let it grow. You would not dare: you would marry a rich man's daughter because you would be afraid of what other people would say of you.

SERGIUS [*bounding up*] You lie: it is not so, by all the stars! If I loved you, and I were the Czar himself, I would set you on the throne by my side. You know that I love another woman, a woman as high above you as heaven is above earth. And you are jealous of her.

LOUKA: I have no reason to be. She will never marry you now. The man I told you of has come back. She will marry the Swiss.

SERGIUS [*recoiling*] The Swiss!

LOUKA: A man worth ten of you. Then you can come to me; and I will refuse you. You are not good enough for me. [*She turns to the door*].

SERGIUS [*springing after her and catching her fiercely in his arms*] I will kill the Swiss; and afterwards I will do as I please with you.

LOUKA [*in his arms, passive and steadfast*] The Swiss will kill you, perhaps. He has beaten you in love. He may beat you in war.

SERGIUS [*tormentedly*] Do you think I believe that she—she! whose worst thoughts are higher than your best ones, is capable of trifling with another man behind my back?

LOUKA: Do you think she would believe the Swiss if he told her now that I am in your arms?

SERGIUS [*releasing her in despair*] Damnation! Oh, damnation! Mockery! mockery everywhere! everything I think is mocked by everything I do. [*He strikes himself frantically on the breast*]. Coward! liar! fool! Shall I kill myself like a man, or live and pretend to laugh at myself? [*She again turns to go*]. Louka! [*She stops near the door*]. Remember: you belong to me.

LOUKA [*turning*] What does that mean? An insult?

SERGIUS [*commandingly*] It means that you love me, and that I have had you here in my arms, and will perhaps have you there again. Whether that is an insult I neither know nor care: take it as you please. But [*vehemently*] I will not be a coward and a trifler. If I choose to love you, I dare marry you, in spite of all Bulgaria. If these hands ever touch you again, they shall touch my affianced bride.

LOUKA: We shall see whether you dare keep your word. And take care. I will not wait long.

SERGIUS [*again folding his arms and standing motionless in the middle of the room*] Yes: we shall see. And you shall wait my pleasure.

Bluntschli, much preoccupied, with his papers still in his hand, enters, leaving the door open for Louka to go out. He goes across to the table, glancing at her as he passes. Sergius, without altering his resolute attitude, watches him steadily. Louka goes out, leaving the door open.

BLUNTSCHLI [*absently, sitting at the table as before, and putting down his papers*] Thats a remarkable looking young woman.

SERGIUS [*gravely, without moving*] Captain Bluntschli.

BLUNTSCHLI: Eh?

SERGIUS: You have deceived me. You are my rival. I brook no rivals. At six o'clock I shall be in the drilling-ground on the Klissoura road, alone, on horseback, with my sabre. Do you understand?

BLUNTSCHLI [*staring, but sitting quite at his ease*] Oh, thank you: thats a cavalry man's proposal. I'm in the artillery; and I have the choice of weapons. If I go, I shall take a machine gun. And there shall be no mistake about the cartridges this time.

SERGIUS [*flushing, but with deadly coldness*] Take care, sir. It is not our custom in Bulgaria to allow invitations of that kind to be trifled with.

BLUNTSCHLI [*warmly*] Pooh! dont talk to me about Bulgaria. You dont know what fighting is. But have it your own way. Bring your sabre along. I'll meet you.

SERGIUS [*fiercely delighted to find his opponent a man of spirit*] Well said, Switzer. Shall I lend you my best horse?

BLUNTSCHLI: No: damn your horse! thank you all the same, my dear fellow. [*Raina comes in, and hears the next sentence*]. I shall fight you on foot. Horseback's too dangerous: I dont want to kill you if I can help it.

RAINA [*hurrying forward anxiously*] I have heard what Captain Bluntschli said, Sergius. You are going to fight. Why? [*Sergius turns away in silence, and goes to the stove, where he stands watching her as she continues, to Bluntschli*] What about?

BLUNTSCHLI: I dont know: he hasnt told me. Better not interfere, dear young lady. No harm will be done: Ive often acted as sword instructor. He wont be able to touch me; and I'll not hurt him. It will save explanations. In the morning I shall be off home; and youll never see me or hear of me again. You and he will then make it up and live happily ever after.

RAINA [*turning away deeply hurt, almost with a sob in her voice*] I never said I wanted to see you again.

SERGIUS [*striding forward*] Ha! That is a confession.

RAINA [*haughtily*] What do you mean?

SERGIUS: You love that man!

RAINA [*scandalized*] Sergius!

SERGIUS: You allow him to make love to you behind my back, just as you treat me as your affianced husband behind his. Bluntschli: you knew our relations; and you deceived me. It is for that that I call you to account, not for having received favors *I* never enjoyed.

BLUNTSCHLI [*jumping up indignantly*] Stuff! Rubbish! I have received no favors. Why, the young lady doesnt even know whether I'm married or not.

RAINA [*forgetting herself*] Oh! [*Collapsing on the ottoman*] Are you?

SERGIUS: You see the young lady's concern, Captain Bluntschli. Denial is useless. You have enjoyed the privilege of being received in her own room, late at night—

BLUNTSCHLI [*interrupting him pepperily*] Yes, you blockhead! she received me with a pistol at her head. Your cavalry were at my heels. I'd have blown out her brains if she'd uttered a cry.

SERGIUS [*taken aback*] Bluntschli! Raina: is this true?

RAINA [*rising in wrathful majesty*] Oh, how dare you, how dare you?

BLUNTSCHLI: Apologize, man: apologize. [*He resumes his seat at the table*].

SERGIUS [*with the old measured emphasis, folding his arms*] I never apologize!

RAINA [*passionately*] This is the doing of that friend of yours, Captain Bluntschli. It is he who is spreading this horrible story about me. [*She walks about excitedly*].

BLUNTSCHLI: No: he's dead. Burnt alive.

RAINA [*stopping, shocked*] Burnt alive!

BLUNTSCHLI: Shot in the hip in a woodyard. Couldnt drag himself out. Your fellows' shells set the timber on fire and burnt him, with half a dozen other poor devils in the same predicament.

RAINA: How horrible!

SERGIUS: And how ridiculous! Oh, war! war! the dream of patriots and heroes! A fraud, Bluntschli. A hollow sham, like love.

RAINA [*outraged*] Like love! You say that before me!

BLUNTSCHLI: Come, Saranoff: that matter is explained.

SERGIUS: A hollow sham, I say. Would you have come back here if nothing had passed between you except at the muzzle of your pistol? Raina is mistaken about your friend who was burnt. He was not my informant.

RAINA: Who then? [*Suddenly guessing the truth*] Ah, Louka! my maid! my servant! You were with her this morning all that time after—after—Oh, what sort of god is this I have been worshipping! [*He meets her gaze with sardonic enjoyment of her disenchantment. Angered all the more, she goes closer to him, and says, in a lower, intenser tone*] Do you know that I looked out of the window as I went upstairs, to have another sight of my hero; and I saw something I did not understand then. I know now that you were making love to her.

SERGIUS [*with grim humor*] You saw that?

RAINA: Only too well. [*She turns away, and throws herself on the divan under the centre window, quite overcome*].

SERGIUS [*cynically*] Raina: our romance is shattered. Life's a farce.

BLUNTSCHLI [*to Raina, whimsically*] You see: he's found himself out now.

SERGIUS [*going to him*] Bluntschli: I have allowed you to call me a blockhead. You may now call me a coward as well. I refuse to fight you. Do you know why?

BLUNTSCHLI: No; but it doesnt matter. I didnt ask the reason when you cried on; and I dont ask the reason now that you cry off. I'm a professional soldier! I fight when I have to, and am very glad to get out of it when I havnt to. Youre only an amateur: you think fighting's an amusement.

SERGIUS [*sitting down at the table, nose to nose with him*] You shall hear the reason all the same, my professional. The reason is that it takes two men—real men—men of heart, blood and honor—to make a genuine combat. I could no more fight with you than I could make love to an ugly woman. Youve no magnetism: youre not a man: youre a machine.

BLUNTSCHLI [*apologetically*] Quite true, quite true. I always was that sort of chap. I'm very sorry.

SERGIUS: Psha!

BLUNTSCHLI: But now that youve found that life isnt a farce, but something quite sensible and serious, what further obstacle is there to your happiness?

RAINA [*rising*] You are very solicitous about my happiness and his. Do you forget his new love—Louka? It is not you that he must fight now, but his rival, Nicola.

SERGIUS: Rival!! [*bounding half across the room*].

RAINA: Dont you know that theyre engaged?

SERGIUS: Nicola! Are fresh abysses opening? Nicola!!

RAINA [*sarcastically*] A shocking sacrifice, isnt it? Such beauty! such intellect! such modesty! wasted on a middle-aged servant man. Really, Sergius, you cannot stand by and allow such a thing. It would be unworthy of your chivalry.

SERGIUS [*losing all self-control*] Viper! Viper! [*He rushes to and fro, raging*].

BLUNTSCHLI: Look here, Saranoff: youre getting the worst of this.

RAINA [*getting angrier*] Do you realize what he has done, Captain Bluntschli? He has set this girl as a spy on us; and her reward is that he makes love to her.

SERGIUS: False! Monstrous!

RAINA: Monstrous! [*Confronting him*] Do you deny that she told you about Captain Bluntschli being in my room?

SERGIUS: No; but—

RAINA [*interrupting*] Do you deny that you were making love to her when she told you?

SERGIUS: No; but I tell you—

RAINA [*cutting him short contemptuously*] It is unnecessary to tell us anything more. That is quite enough for us. [*She turns away from him and sweeps majestically back to the window*].

BLUNTSCHLI [*quietly, as Sergius, in an agony of mortification, sinks on the ottoman, clutching his averted head between his fists*] I told you you were getting the worst of it, Saranoff.

SERGIUS: Tiger cat!

RAINA [*running excitedly to Bluntschli*] You hear this man calling me names, Captain Bluntschli?

BLUNTSCHLI: What else can he do, dear lady? He must defend himself somehow. Come [*very persuasively*]: dont quarrel. What good does it do?

Raina, with a gasp, sits down on the ottoman, and after a vain effort to look vexedly at Bluntschli, falls a victim to her sense of humor, and actually leans back babyishly against the writhing shoulder of Sergius.

SERGIUS: Engaged to Nicola! Ha! ha! Ah well, Bluntschli, you are right to take this huge imposture of a world coolly.

RAINA [*quaintly to Bluntschli, with an intuitive guess at his state of mind*] I daresay you think us a couple of grown-up babies, dont you?

SERGIUS [*grinning savagely*] He does: he does. Swiss civilization nursetending Bulgarian barbarism, eh?

BLUNTSCHLI [*blushing*] Not at all, I assure you. I'm only very glad to get you two quieted. There! there! let's be pleasant and talk it over in a friendly way. Where is this other young lady?

RAINA: Listening at the door, probably.

SERGIUS [*shivering as if a bullet had struck him, and speaking with quiet but deep indignation*] I will prove that that, at least, is a calumny. [*He goes with dignity to the door and opens it. A yell of fury bursts from him as he looks out. He darts into the passage, and returns dragging in Louka, whom he flings violently against the table, exclaiming*] Judge her, Bluntschli. You, the cool impartial man: judge the eavesdropper.

Louka stands her ground, proud and silent.

BLUNTSCHLI [*shaking his head*] I mustnt judge her. I once listened myself outside a tent when there was a mutiny brewing. It's all a question of the degree of provocation. My life was at stake.

LOUKA: My love was at stake. I am not ashamed.

RAINA [*contemptuously*] Your love! Your curiosity, you mean.

LOUKA [*facing her and retorting her contempt with interest*] My love, stronger than anything you can feel, even for your chocolate cream soldier.

SERGIUS [*with quick suspicion, to Louka*] What does that mean?

LOUKA [*fiercely*] It means—

SERGIUS [*interrupting her slightingly*] Oh, I remember: the ice pudding. A paltry taunt, girl!

Major Petkoff enters, in his shirtsleeves.

PETKOFF: Excuse my shirtsleeves, gentlemen. Raina: somebody has been wearing that coat of mine: I'll swear it. Somebody with a differently shaped back. It's all burst open at the sleeve. Your mother is mending it. I wish she'd make haste: I shall catch cold. [*He looks more attentively at them*]. Is anything the matter?

RAINA: No. [*She sits down at the stove, with a tranquil air*].

SERGIUS: Oh no. [*He sits down at the end of the table, as at first*].

BLUNTSCHLI [*who is already seated*] Nothing. Nothing.

PETKOFF [*sitting down on the ottoman in his old place*] Thats all right. [*He notices Louka*]. Anything the matter, Louka?

LOUKA: No, sir.

PETKOFF [*genially*] Thats all right. [*He sneezes*] Go and ask your mistress for my coat, like a good girl, will you?

Nicola enters with the coat. Louka makes a pretence of hav-

ing business in the room by taking the little table with the hookah away to the wall near the windows.

RAINA [*rising quickly as she sees the coat on Nicola's arm*] Here it is papa. Give it to me Nicola; and do you put some more wood on the fire. [*She takes the coat, and brings it to the Major, who stands up to put it on. Nicola attends to the fire*].

PETKOFF [*to Raina, teasing her affectionately*] Aha! Going to be very good to poor old papa just for one day after his return from the wars, eh?

RAINA [*with solemn reproach*] Ah, how can you say that to me, father?

PETKOFF: Well, well, only a joke, little one. Come: give me a kiss. [*She kisses him*]. Now give me the coat.

RAINA: No: I am going to put it on for you. Turn your back. [*He turns his back and feels behind him with his arms for the sleeves. She dexterously takes the photograph from the pocket and throws it on the table before Bluntschli, who covers it with a sheet of paper under the very nose of Sergius, who looks on amazed, with his suspicions roused in the highest degree. She then helps Petkoff on with his coat*]. There, dear! Now are you comfortable?

PETKOFF: Quite, little love. Thanks [*He sits down; and Raina returns to her seat near the stove*]. Oh, by the bye, Ive found something funny. Whats the meaning of this? [*He puts his hand into the picked pocket*]. Eh? Hallo! [*He tries the other pocket*]. Well, I could have sworn—! [*Much puzzled, he tries the breast pocket*]. I wonder—[*trying the original pocket*]. Where can it—? [*He rises, exclaiming*] Your mother's taken it!

RAINA [*very red*] Taken what?

PETKOFF: Your photograph, with the inscription: "Raina, to her Chocolate Cream Soldier: a Souvenir." Now you know theres something more in this than meets the eye; and I'm going to find it out. [*Shouting*] Nicola!

NICOLA [*coming to him*] Sir!

PETKOFF: Did you spoil any pastry of Miss Raina's this morning?

NICOLA: You heard Miss Raina say that I did, sir.

PETKOFF: I know that, you idiot. Was it true?

NICOLA: I am sure Miss Raina is incapable of saying anything that is not true, sir.

PETKOFF: Are you? Then I'm not. [*Turning to the others*] Come: do you think I dont see it all? [*He goes to Sergius, and slaps him on the shoulder*]. Sergius: youre the chocolate cream soldier, arnt you?

SERGIUS [*starting up*] I! A chocolate cream soldier! Certainly not.

PETKOFF: Not! [*He looks at them. They are all very serious and very conscious*]. Do you mean to tell me that Raina sends things like that to other men?

SERGIUS [*enigmatically*] The world is not such an innocent place as we used to think, Petkoff.

BLUNTSCHLI [*rising*] It's all right, Major. I'm the chocolate cream soldier. [*Petkoff and Sergius are equally astonished*]. The gracious young lady saved my life by giving me chocolate creams when I was starving: shall I ever forget their flavour! My late friend Stolz told you the story at Pirot. I was the fugitive.

PETKOFF: You! [*He gasps*]. Sergius: do you remember how those two women went on this morning when we mentioned it? [*Sergius smiles cynically. Petkoff confronts Raina severely*]. Youre a nice young woman, arnt you?

RAINA [*bitterly*] Major Saranoff has changed his mind. And when I wrote that on the photograph, I did not know that Captain Bluntschli was married.

BLUNTSCHLI [*startled into vehement protest*] I'm not married.

RAINA [*with deep reproach*] You said you were.

BLUNTSCHLI: I did not. I positively did not. I never was married in my life.

PETKOFF [*exasperated*] Raina: will you kindly inform me, if I am not asking too much, which of these gentlemen you are engaged to?

RAINA: To neither of them. This young lady [*introducing Louka, who faces them all proudly*] is the object of Major Saranoff's affections at present.

PETKOFF: Louka! Are you mad, Sergius? Why, this girl's engaged to Nicola.

NICOLA: I beg your pardon, sir. There is a mistake. Louka is not engaged to me.

PETKOFF: Not engaged to you, you scoundrel! Why, you had twenty-five levas from me on the day of your betrothal; and she had that gilt bracelet from Miss Raina.

NICOLA [*with cool unction*] We gave it out so, sir. But it was only to give Louka protection. She had a soul above her station; and I have been no more than her confidential servant. I intend, as you know, sir, to set up a shop later on in Sofia; and I look forward to her custom and recommendation should she marry into the nobility. [*He goes out with impressive discretion, leaving them all staring after him*].

PETKOFF [*breaking the silence*] Well, I am—hm!

SERGIUS: This is either the finest heroism or the most crawling baseness. Which is it, Bluntschli?

BLUNTSCHLI: Never mind whether it's heroism or baseness. Nicola's the ablest man Ive met in Bulgaria. I'll make him manager of a hotel if he can speak French and German.

LOUKA [*suddenly breaking out at Sergius*] I have been insulted by everyone here. You set them the example. You owe me an apology.

Sergius, *like a repeating clock of which the spring has been touched, immediately begins to fold his arms.*

BLUNTSCHLI [*before he can speak*] It's no use. He never apologizes.

LOUKA: Not to you, his equal and his enemy. To me, his poor servant, he will not refuse to apologize.

SERGIUS [*approvingly*] You are right. [*He bends his knee in his grandest manner*] Forgive me.

LOUKA: I forgive you. [*She timidly gives him her hand, which he kisses*]. That touch makes me your affianced wife.

SERGIUS [*springing up*] Ah! I forgot that.

LOUKA [*coldly*] You can withdraw if you like.

SERGIUS: Withdraw! Never! You belong to me. [*He puts his arm about her*].

Catherine comes in and finds Louka in Sergius's arms, with all the rest gazing at them in bewildered astonishment.

CATHERINE: What does this mean?

Sergius releases Louka.

PETKOFF: Well, my dear, it appears that Sergius is going to marry Louka instead of Raina. [*She is about to break out indignantly at him: he stops her by exclaiming testily*] Dont blame me: Ive nothing to do with it. [*He retreats to the stove*].

CATHERINE: Marry Louka! Sergius: you are bound by your word to us!

SERGIUS [*folding his arms*] Nothing binds me.

BLUNTSCHLI [*much pleased by this piece of common sense*] Saranoff: your hand. My congratulations. These heroics of yours have their practical side after all. [*To Louka*] Gracious young lady: the best wishes of a good Republican! [*He kisses her hand, to Raina's great disgust, and returns to his seat*].

CATHERINE: Louka: you have been telling stories.

LOUKA: I have done Raina no harm.

CATHERINE [*haughtily*] Raina!

Raina, equally indignant, almost snorts at the liberty.

LOUKA: I have a right to call her Raina: she calls me Louka. I told Major Saranoff she would never marry him if the Swiss gentleman came back.

BLUNTSCHLI [*rising, much surprised*] Hallo!

LOUKA [*turning to Raina*] I thought you were fonder of him than of Sergius. You know best whether I was right.

BLUNTSCHLI: What nonsense! I assure you, my dear Major, my dear Madam, the gracious young lady simply saved my life, nothing else. She never cared two straws for me. Why, bless my heart and soul, look at the young lady and look at me. She, rich, young, beautiful, with her imagination full of fairy princes and noble natures and cavalry charges and goodness knows what! And I, a commonplace Swiss soldier who hardly knows what a decent life is after fifteen years of barracks and battles: a vagabond, a man who has spoiled all his chances in life through an incurably romantic disposition, a man—

SERGIUS [*starting as if a needle had pricked him and interrupting Bluntschli in incredulous amazement*] Excuse me, Bluntschli: what did you say had spoiled your chances in life?

BLUNTSCHLI [*promptly*] An incurably romantic disposition. I ran away from home twice when I was a boy. I went into the army instead of into my father's business. I climbed the balcony of this house when a man of sense would have dived into the nearest cellar. I came sneaking back here to have another look at the young lady when any other man of my age would have sent the coat back—

PETKOFF: My coat!

BLUNTSCHLI: —yes: thats the coat I mean—would have sent it back and gone quietly home. Do you suppose I am the sort of fellow a young girl falls in love with? Why, look at our ages! I'm thirty-four: I dont suppose the young lady is much over seventeen. [*This estimate produces a marked sensation, all the rest turning and staring at one another. He proceeds innocently*] All that adventure which was life or death to me, was only a schoolgirl's game to her—chocolate creams and hide and seek. Heres the proof! [*He takes the photograph from the table*]. Now, I ask you, would a woman who took the affair seriously have sent me this and written on it "Raina, to her Chocolate Cream Soldier: a Souvenir"? [*He exhibits the photograph triumphantly, as if it settled the matter beyond all possibility of refutation*].

PETKOFF: Thats what I was looking for. How the deuce did it get there? [*He comes from the stove to look at it, and sits down on the ottoman*].

BLUNTSCHLI [*to Raina, complacently*] I have put everything right, I hope, gracious young lady.

RAINA [*going to the table to face him*] I quite agree with your account of yourself. You are a romantic idiot. [*Bluntschli is unspeakably taken aback*]. Next time, I hope you will know the difference between a schoolgirl of seventeen and a woman of twenty-three.

BLUNTSCHLI [*stupefied*] Twenty-three!

Raina snaps the photograph contemptuously from his hand; tears it up; throws the pieces in his face; and sweeps back to her former place.

SERGIUS [*with grim enjoyment of his rival's discomfiture*] Bluntschli: my one last belief is gone. Your sagacity is a fraud, like everything else. You have less sense than even I!

BLUNTSCHLI [*overwhelmed*] Twenty-three! Twenty-three!! [*He considers*]. Hm! [*Swiftly making up his mind and coming to his host*] In that case, Major Petkoff, I beg to propose formally to become a suitor for your daughter's hand, in place of Major Saranoff retired.

RAINA: You dare!

BLUNTSCHLI: If you were twenty-three when you said those things to me this afternoon, I shall take them seriously.

CATHERINE [*loftily polite*] I doubt, sir, whether you quite realize either my daughter's position or that of Major Sergius Saranoff, whose place you propose to take. The Petkoffs and the Saranoffs are known as the richest and most important families in the country. Our position is almost historical: we can go back for twenty years.

PETKOFF: Oh, never mind that, Catherine. [*To Bluntschli*] We should be most happy, Bluntschli, if it were only a question of your position; but hang it, you know, Raina is accustomed to a very comfortable establishment. Sergius keeps twenty horses.

BLUNTSCHLI: But who wants twenty horses? We're not going to keep a circus.

CATHERINE [*severely*] My daughter, sir, is accustomed to a first-rate stable.

RAINA: Hush, mother: youre making me ridiculous.

BLUNTSCHLI: Oh well, if it comes to a question of an establishment, here goes! [*He darts impetuously to the table; seizes the papers in the blue envelope; and turns to Sergius*]. How many horses did you say?

SERGIUS: Twenty, noble Switzer.

BLUNTSCHLI: I have two hundred horses. [*They are amazed*]. How many carriages?

SERGIUS: Three.

BLUNTSCHLI: I have seventy. Twenty-four of them will hold twelve inside, besides two on the box, without counting the driver and conductor. How many tablecloths have you?

SERGIUS: How the deuce do I know?

BLUNTSCHLI: Have you four thousand?

SERGIUS: No.

BLUNTSCHLI: I have. I have nine thousand six hundred pairs of sheets and blankets, with two thousand four hundred eider-down quilts. I have ten thousand knives and forks, and the same quantity of dessert spoons. I have three hundred servants. I have six palatial establishments, besides two livery stables, a tea gardens, and a private house. I have four medals for distinguished services; I have the rank of an officer and the standing of a gentleman; and I have three native languages. Shew me any man in Bulgaria that can offer as much!

PETKOFF [with childish awe] Are you Emperor of Switzerland?

BLUNTSCHLI: My rank is the highest known in Switzerland: I am a free citizen.

CATHERINE: Then, Captain Bluntschli, since you are my daughter's choice—

RAINA [mutinously] He's not.

CATHERINE [ignoring her]—I shall not stand in the way of her happiness. [Petkoff is about to speak] That is Major Petkoff's feeling also.

PETKOFF: Oh, I shall be only too glad. Two hundred horses! Whew!

SERGIUS: What says the lady?

RAINA [pretending to sulk] The lady says that he can keep his tablecloths and his omnibuses. I am not here to be sold to the highest bidder. [She turns her back on him].

BLUNTSCHLI: I wont take that answer. I appealed to you as a fugitive, a beggar, and a starving man. You accepted me. You gave me your hand to kiss, your bed to sleep in, and your roof to shelter me.

RAINA: I did not give them to the Emperor of Switzerland.

BLUNTSCHLI: Thats just what I say. [He catches her by the

shoulders and turns her face-to-face with him]. Now tell us whom you did give them to.

RAINA [*succumbing with a shy smile*] To my chocolate cream soldier.

BLUNTSCHLI [*with a boyish laugh of delight*] Thatll do. Thank you. [*He looks at his watch and suddenly becomes businesslike*]. Time's up, Major. Youve managed those regiments so well that youre sure to be asked to get rid of some of the infantry of the Timok division. Send them home by way of Lom Palanka. Saranoff: dont get married until I come back: I shall be here punctually at five in the evening on Tuesday fortnight. Gracious ladies [*his heels click*] good evening. [*He makes them a military bow, and goes*].

SERGIUS: What a man! Is he a man!

Composition and Cast List

Composition begun 26 November 1893; completed 30 March 1894. Published in *Plays Pleasant and Unpleasant,* 1898. Revised text in *Collected Edition,* 1930. First presented by Florence Farr at the Avenue Theatre, London, on 21 April 1894 (fifty performances).

MAJOR PAUL PETKOFF   *James Welch*
MAJOR SERGIUS SARANOFF   *Bernard Gould*
CAPTAIN BLUNTSCHLI   *Yorke Stephens*
MAJOR PLECHANOFF   *A. E. W. Mason*
NICOLA   *Orlando Barnett*
CATHERINE PETKOFF   *Mrs. Charles Calvert*
RAINA PETKOFF   *Alma Murray*
LOUKA   *Florence Farr*

The action occurs at Major Petkoff's house in a small Bulgarian town, near the Dragoman Pass, 1885–86.

ACT I   *Raina's Chamber*
ACT II   *The Garden*
ACT III   *The Library*

The Bernard Shaw Library featuring the definitive texts prepared
under the editorial supervision of Dan H. Laurence

Arms and the Man
Introduction by Rodelle Weintraub
Raina, a young Bulgarian woman with romantic notions of war and an idealized
view of her soldier fiancé, is surprised one night by a Swiss mercenary soldier
seeking refuge in her bedchamber. The pragmatic Captain Bluntschli proceeds, in
the course of one of Shaw's most delightful comedies, to puncture all of Raina's
illusions about love, heroism, and class. Optimistic, farcical, absurd, and teeming
with sexual energy, *Arms and the Man* has Shaw inverting the devices of melodrama to glorious effect.   ISBN 0-14-303976-8

Caesar and Cleopatra
Introduction by Stanley Weintraub
In a cheeky nod to Shakespeare's towering reputation, Shaw reinvents two of his
historical characters but sets his own play in a period predating both *Julius Caesar*
and *Antony and Cleopatra*. Shaw's Cleopatra is kittenish girl with a streak of cruelty, while his Caesar is a world-weary philosopher-soldier who is as much a
stranger in Rome as in the barbaric court of Egypt. With wit and irony, *Caesar
and Cleopatra* satirizes Shakespeare's use of history and comments wryly on the
politics of Shaw's own time. With its undertone of melancholy, it is one of his
most affecting plays.   ISBN 0-14-303977-6

Candida
Introduction by Peter Gahan
The Reverend Morell, a Socialist preacher, brings a young penniless poet, Eugene
Marchbanks, into his home, which is dominated by his fascinating wife, Candida.
With its single stage setting and small cast of six characters, this play of Shaw's is
deceptively simple. Centered on a romantic triangle and parodying courtly love
and the domestic drama of Ibsen, *Candida* also abounds with classical allusions,
the fervor of a religious revival, and poetic inspiration and aspirations.
                                                          ISBN 0-14-303978-4

Heartbreak House
Introduction by David Hare
Set during a house party at the eccentric household of Captain Shotover and his
daughter Hesione, this comedy of manners takes a probing look at the conflict
between "old-fashioned" idealism and the realities of the modern age. *Heartbreak
House* was Shaw's own favorite play.   ISBN 0-14-043787-8

Major Barbara
Introduction by Margery Morgan
In this sparkling comedy, Andrew Undershaft is a millionaire armaments dealer
obsessed with money and hostile toward the poor. His energetic daughter
Barbara, however, is a devout major in the Salvation Army. She sees her father as
just another soul to be saved. But when the Salvation Army needs funds to keep
going, it is Undershaft who saves the day.   ISBN 0-14-043790-8

Man and Superman
Introduction by Stanley Weintraub
John Tanner, author of *The Revolutionist's Handbook*, is horrified to discover that Ann Whitefield intends to marry him and flees, with the young woman in hot pursuit, on a chase that eventually leads to the underworld. A wonderfully original twist on the Don Juan myth, this finely tuned combination of intellectual seriousness and popular comedy is a classic exposé of the eternal struggle between the sexes.
ISBN 0-14-043788-6

Pygmalion
Introduction by Nicholas Grene
Shaw radically reworks Ovid's tale to give it a feminist slant: While Henry Higgins successfully teaches Eliza to speak and act like a duchess, she asserts her independence, adamantly refusing to be his creation. A brilliantly witty exposure of the British class system, the exceedingly entertaining *Pygmalion* remains one of Shaw's most popular plays.
ISBN 0-14-143950-5

Saint Joan
Introduction by Joley Wood
"On Playing Joan" by Imogen Stubbs
With *Saint Joan*, Shaw reached the height of his fame as a dramatist. Fascinated by the story of Joan of Arc (canonized in 1920), but unhappy with "the whitewash which disfigures her beyond recognition," he presents a realistic Joan: proud, intolerant, naive, foolhardy, always brave—a rebel who challenged the conventions and values of her day.
ISBN 0-14-043791-6

Plays Pleasant
Introduction by W. J. McCormack
Plays Pleasant comprises four comedies intended not only to amuse audiences but also to provoke them. *Arms and the Man*, set in the Balkan mountains, satirizes romantic views of war and military heroism. *Candida* presents the complicated relationship between a vicar, his wife, and her young admirer. *The Man of Destiny* is a witty war of words between a "strange lady" and a Napoleon Bonaparte at odds with English mores. The exuberant farce *You Never Can Tell* presents an aging suffragette and a divided family reunited by chance. *ISBN 0-14-043794-0*

Plays Unpleasant
Introduction by David Edgar
With *Plays Unpleasant*, Shaw broke all the rules governing how a playwright should entertain his audience. In *Widowers' Houses*, Harry Trench's engagement to Blanche Sartorius is called into question when he realizes that her father is a slum landlord. In *The Philanderer*, charismatic Leonard Charteris proposes marriage to Grace while still involved with the beautiful Julia Craven—but Julia is not inclined to surrender him so easily. And in *Mrs. Warren's Profession*, Vivie must reconsider her own life when she discovers that her mother's immoral earnings have paid for her genteel upbringing.
ISBN 0-14-043793-2

Three Plays for Puritans
Introduction by Michael Billington
Disgusted and bored by the trend for titillation and sham on the London stage, Shaw wrote these plays both to educate and to entertain his audiences. In *The Devil's Disciple*, a clergyman turned soldier—the Shavian ideal of a Puritan hero—willingly risks his life for a stranger. The brilliant historical satire *Caesar and Cleopatra* contains unexpected portraits of its title characters. In *Captain Brassbound's Conversion*, it is Lady Cicely's cunning manipulation of the truth that ensures that fairness, rather than justice, prevails. *ISBN 0-14-043792-4*

CLICK ON A CLASSIC
www.penguinclassics.com

The world's greatest literature at your fingertips

Constantly updated information on more than a thousand titles,
from Icelandic sagas to ancient Indian epics, Russian drama to
Italian romance, American greats to African masterpieces

•

The latest news on recent additions to the list, updated
editions, and specially commissioned translations

•

Original essays by leading writers

•

A wealth of background material, including biographies
of every classic author from Aristotle to Zamyatin, plot
synopses, readers' and teachers' guides, useful web links

•

Online desk and examination copy assistance for academics

•

Trivia quizzes, competitions, giveaways, news on
forthcoming screen adaptations

FOR THE BEST IN PAPERBACKS, LOOK FOR THE 🐧

In every corner of the world, on every subject under the sun, Penguin represents quality and variety—the very best in publishing today.

For complete information about books available from Penguin—including Penguin Classics, Penguin Compass, and Puffins—and how to order them, write to us at the appropriate address below. Please note that for copyright reasons the selection of books varies from country to country.

In the United States: Please write to *Penguin Group (USA), P.O. Box 12289 Dept. B, Newark, New Jersey 07101-5289* or call 1-800-788-6262.

In the United Kingdom: Please write to *Dept. EP, Penguin Books Ltd, Bath Road, Harmondsworth, West Drayton, Middlesex UB7 0DA.*

In Canada: Please write to *Penguin Books Canada Ltd, 90 Eglinton Avenue East, Suite 700, Toronto, Ontario M4P 2Y3.*

In Australia: Please write to *Penguin Books Australia Ltd, P.O. Box 257, Ringwood, Victoria 3134.*

In New Zealand: Please write to *Penguin Books (NZ) Ltd, Private Bag 102902, North Shore Mail Centre, Auckland 10.*

In India: Please write to *Penguin Books India Pvt Ltd, 11 Panchsheel Shopping Centre, Panchsheel Park, New Delhi 110 017.*

In the Netherlands: Please write to *Penguin Books Netherlands bv, Postbus 3507, NL-1001 AH Amsterdam.*

In Germany: Please write to *Penguin Books Deutschland GmbH, Metzlerstrasse 26, 60594 Frankfurt am Main.*

In Spain: Please write to *Penguin Books S. A., Bravo Murillo 19, 1° B, 28015 Madrid.*

In Italy: Please write to *Penguin Italia s.r.l., Via Benedetto Croce 2, 20094 Corsico, Milano.*

In France: Please write to *Penguin France, Le Carré Wilson, 62 rue Benjamin Baillaud, 31500 Toulouse.*

In Japan: Please write to *Penguin Books Japan Ltd, Kaneko Building, 2-3-25 Koraku, Bunkyo-Ku, Tokyo 112.*

In South Africa: Please write to *Penguin Books South Africa (Pty) Ltd, Private Bag X14, Parkview, 2122 Johannesburg.*